20 | 8 | 13

30p

# IBIZA

Thomas Cook

Written by Mike Gerrard, updated by Victoria Trott

Published by Thomas Cook Publishing
A division of Thomas Cook Tour Operations Limited
Company registration no. 3772199 England
The Thomas Cook Business Park, Unit 9, Coningsby Road
Peterborough PE3 8SB, United Kingdom
Email: books@thomascook.com, Tel: + 44 (0) 1733 416477
www.thomascookpublishing.com

Produced by Cambridge Publishing Management Limited
Burr Elm Court, Main Street, Caldecote CB23 7NU

ISBN: 978-1-84848-255-5

© 2006, 2008 Thomas Cook Publishing
This third edition © 2010
Text © Thomas Cook Publishing
Maps © Thomas Cook Publishing/PCGraphics (UK) Limited

Series Editor: Adam Royal
Production/DTP: Steven Collins

Printed and bound in Spain by GraphyCems

Cover photography © Thomas Cook

# CONTENTS

## WHAT'S IN YOUR GUIDEBOOK?

**Independent authors** Impartial, up-to-date information from our travel experts who meticulously source local knowledge.

**Experience** Thomas Cook's 165 years in the travel industry and guidebook publishing enriches every word with expertise you can trust.

**Travel know-how** Contributions by thousands of staff around the globe, each one living and breathing travel.

**Editors** Travel-publishing professionals, pulling everything together to craft a perfect blend of words, pictures, maps and design.

**You, the traveller** We deliver a practical, no-nonsense approach to information, geared to how you really use it.

▶ *The whitewashed village of Santa Eulària*

# INTRODUCTION
Getting to know Ibiza

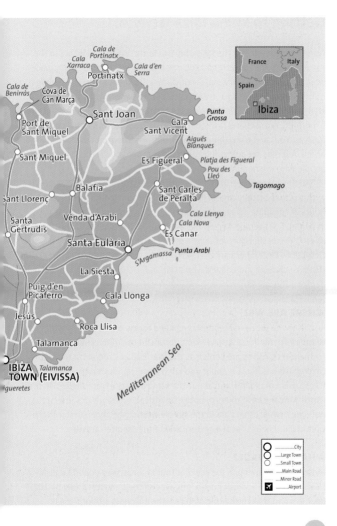

# Getting to know Ibiza (Eivissa)

Artists discovered it in the 1950s, hippies in the 1960s, the jet set in the 1970s, and by the 1990s it had become the biggest all-night party place in Europe. Now Ibiza (Eivissa) is reinventing itself yet again by opening a number of upmarket country retreats (*agroturismos*) with spas and stylish lounge bars. This little jewel of an island is home to film stars and fishermen, farmers and fashion models, DJs and dancers, expats and tourists. You can be anything on Ibiza, but one thing you won't be is bored. You may see some outrageous things, yet you can be sure that the people who live here have seen it all before.

All this takes place on an island about the size of the Isle of Man – with a rather better climate! Ibiza boasts 300 sunny days a year, with ten hours of sunshine a day in the summer, and five hours a day most days in winter. The average August has 31 sunny days in a row, but this doesn't mean that it never rains – most of the rainfall saves itself for the October to December period. However, even if there's a freak summer storm or shower, you know it won't last and it's never enough to dampen the spirits.

## WHERE ARE WE?

Ibiza is in the western Mediterranean and forms part of the Balearic Islands with Mallorca and Menorca. Ibiza and the much smaller isle of Formentera close by are known as the Islas Pitiüses, meaning the 'pine-covered islands'. Ibiza is about 240 km (150 miles) south of Barcelona on the Spanish mainland, and about the same distance from Algiers on the North African coast. You may notice an African influence in some of the buildings, while others are in the simple white cube style, similar to the Greek Island houses at the eastern end of the Mediterranean.

## WHAT LANGUAGE?

Most people working in the popular tourist areas speak good English. However, a little Spanish goes a long way so try to master a few basics. Bear in mind that the people of Ibiza – the Ibicencos – might speak

Catalan or their local dialect of Catalan, Ibicenco or Eivissenc, or Castilian Spanish. All three languages exist side by side, which can be a little confusing until you get used to it. Road signs are usually in Catalan but maps are often in Spanish, so be prepared for most places to have two slightly different names. Catalan names are used in this book for main resorts. The locals know their own island, and its main town, by the name of Eivissa.

## THE REAL IBIZA
Whether you call it Ibiza or Eivissa, the island is beautiful. It has many lovely sandy beaches, some busy, others quiet and hidden away. Its highest point, Sa Talaia, may only be 475 m (1,560 ft), but you can see the Spanish mainland if you venture to the top on a clear day. This peak is surrounded by some fertile farmland, *salinas* (salt flats), and even that rare thing for a small Mediterranean island: a river. There are villages inland that are almost untouched by tourism, and you should definitely make an effort to explore the interior and meet the people who don't normally meet the tourists.

You'll get an incredibly warm welcome, especially if you venture into a village's only bar or café, or try to buy something in the solitary shop. This is what some people like to call the 'real Ibiza', though the truth is that everywhere on the island is now the 'real Ibiza', from hamlets that are sleepy to bustling resorts that are virtually sleepless.

## PEOPLE & PLACES
Around 133,000 people live on Ibiza, about 47,000 of them in the capital, which is usually known to holidaymakers as Ibiza Town. This is a lively place where everyone finds something to interest them, whether it's the old walled town, Dalt Vila, with its cathedral and museums, the ever-changing bar and club scene, the fishing harbour, the designer shops, the art galleries or the range of restaurants.

However long you think you'll need when you visit Ibiza Town, make it longer. And if you find you haven't had enough of Ibiza by the end of your holiday, you can always come back. Most people do.

# THE BEST OF IBIZA

## TOP 10 ATTRACTIONS

- **Explore the many lovely beaches.** These are some of the most popular: Platja d'en Bossa (see page 23), Cala Tarida and Cala d'Hort (see page 28), Cala Sant Vicent (see page 48) and Es Canar (see page 53). Aigües Blanques (see page 48) on the northeast coast is one of the loveliest beaches on the island.

- **Ibiza is of course famous for its parties and clubbing** and internationally reknowned DJs are brought to its clubs (see page 68).

- **Venture inland to discover** why Ibiza and Formentera were known to Greek traders as the 'pine islands'. Alternatively, rent a car for a few days and see some of the unspoiled island villages, such as Sant Rafel or Sant Carles de Peralta (see page 78).

- **Wander around the Dalt Vila in Ibiza Town** – the medieval town within the ancient walls became a World Heritage Site in 1999 (see page 17).

- **Visit Santa Eulària** – Ibiza's third-largest town combines modern tourism around the port with a traditional seaside atmosphere (see page 63).

- **Take a boat trip to Formentera**, a much more peaceful island that can be explored on a bike, by local bus, by car or on foot (see page 85).

- **Get a taste for the local food**, from paella and sangría to squid, fresh fish and *hierbas*, the local drink that combines alcohol with herbs (see page 93).

- **Visit Ibiza Town at night**, especially La Marina and Sa Penya districts between the city walls and the port. You'll see a parade of people from the beautiful to the extraordinary (see page 15).

- Take in one of the **Hippy Markets**. You'll meet a great mix of locals, hippies, Africans and tourists: a good cross-section of Ibizan life, in fact. One of the biggest is at Es Canar on Wednesdays (see page 54).

- **Watch the sun go down from one of the sunset bars** along the Sunset Strip in San Antonio (see page 37).

⬢ *Dalt Vila seen from the sea*

## SYMBOLS KEY
The following symbols are used throughout this book:

---

**a** address **t** telephone **w** website address **c** opening times

**!** important

---

The following symbols are used on the maps:

**i** information office     ○ city

**✉** post office     ○ large town

**🛍** shopping     ○ small town

**✈** airport     ■ POI (point of interest)

**✚** medical centres     — main road

**♛** police station     — minor road

**🚌** bus station/stop

**✝** church

**❶** numbers denote featured cafés, restaurants & evening venues

---

### RESTAURANT CATEGORIES
Restaurants in this guide are graded by approximate price as follows:
£ = up to €15    ££ = €15–€30    £££ = over €30
This refers to the cost of a meal for two excluding wine, taxes and service.

---

▶ *The picturesque harbour of Ibiza Town*

# RESORTS
## Places under the sun

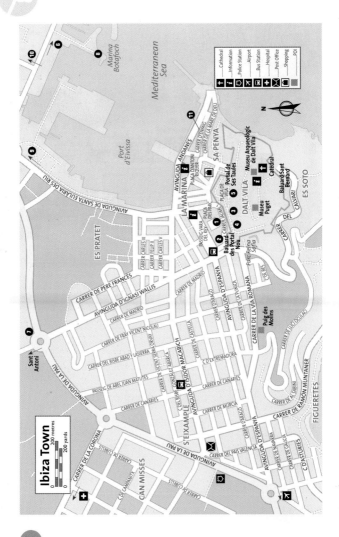

Ibiza Town

0   200 metres
0   200 yards

# Ibiza Town (Eivissa)

A trip to Ibiza's capital, known as Eivissa in Catalan, combining the old city with the modern town, makes a great day out. Stroll around the narrow streets of Sa Penya and La Marina, browse the shops stocked full of souvenirs, stop by the Plaça des Parc for a coffee, or try out one of the many restaurants nearer the port. You'll know when you're close to the port as you will see the high old town, Dalt Vila, clustered around its rock on top of which sits the cathedral.

The medieval town of Dalt Vila sits like a crown above Ibiza Town and should be high on everyone's list of options. Within its ancient walls are several museums and a cathedral, as well as shops and restaurants. It's a great place to stroll – you will almost certainly get lost through the zigzag streets, but that's part of the fun.

One of the best ways to explore this area is to take a taxi (ask the driver for 'Es Soto') and walk down, or to take the *vilabus* from Vara de Rey (or other stops in town) up to the Plaça d'Espanya. It is worth doing this to avoid walking up the steep inclines that can be especially tiring in the heat of the day. Access by car is for residents only. There are three points of entry for pedestrians: at the top of Dalt Vila by the ramp through the Portal de ses Taules; halfway up via the steps at the Baluard des Portal Nou; and south of the town at Baluard Sant Bernard.

At night the area buzzes, with its bars and restaurants attracting an eye-opening cast of characters. Buses from other resorts run until quite late, so you could plan to stay for dinner and have a few drinks, or even spend the evening shopping as most shops stay open until 23.00 in the old part of town.

## THINGS TO SEE & DO

### Boat trips

There are all kinds of boat trips available from the port in Ibiza Town. You can visit other resorts, the Hippy Market in Es Canar (see page 54), the island of Formentera or take a quick hop to Marina Botafoch on the

north side of the port. Spend a few hours visiting nearby bays or charter a yacht for up to 40 people in Marina Botafoch.

### Catedral de Santa María (St Mary's Cathedral)

It is thought that there has been some kind of temple on this site for at least 2,500 years. Parts of the present building, such as the bell tower, date from the 14th century, but most are from the 18th.

ⓐ Plaça de la Catedral ⓣ 971 30 27 23 ⓛ 09.30–13.30 & 17.00–20.00 Mon–Sat, Mass 10.30 Sun

● Ibiza Town (also known as Eivissa)

## Museu Arqueològic de Dalt Vila (Archaeological Museum)

This is worth seeing if you're interested in the history of Ibiza and Formentera; there are good displays and explanations in English.
ⓐ Plaça de la Catedral, next to the cathedral ❶ 971 30 12 31
🕐 10.00–14.00 & 18.00–20.00 Tues–Sun (Apr–Sept); 09.00–15.00 Tues–Sun (Oct–Mar), closed Mon ❶ Admission charge

## Museu Puget

This new museum, opened in 2007, is dedicated to Ibizan artist and photographer Narcís Puget Viñas (1874–1960). The second floor exhibits a number of his paintings, drawings and watercolours of the town and its residents.
ⓐ Palau de Can Comasema, Carrer Sant Ciriac 18 ❶ 971 39 21 37
ⓦ www.museopuget.com 🕐 10.00–13.30 (Tues–Sun), 17.00–20.00 Tues–Fri (May–Sept); 10.00–13.30 Tues–Sun, 16.00–18.00 Tues–Fri (Oct–Apr), closed Mon

## Old Town (Dalt Vila)

Join one of the free 90-minute guided tours. Enquire at the Centro d'Interpretació, Casa de la Curia.

### SHOPPING

**Club Wear** All the major clubs, such as Pacha (see page 20), have shops along the port.
**Fashion/jewellery** La Marina and Sa Penya are the places to look. In addition, there are more shops in **Dalt Vila**, most of them near the **Plaça de Vila**.
**Mango** The same good-quality clothes you'd find in Mango shops at home, but cheaper. ⓐ Carrer Riambau 🕐 11.00–23.00 daily
**Markets** An evening Hippy Market takes place in La Marina. The small fruit and fish market outside the Portal de ses Taules of Dalt Vila (🕐 until 14.00 daily) is worth a visit – ask for *el mercado*.

@ Carrer Major in Dalt Vila ☏ 971 39 92 32 ⓦ www.ibiza.travel/en
🕐 Days & times vary

## Plaça des Parc

This is the centre of Ibizan café culture. Stop for a coffee and watch the activity in the centre of this pleasant palm-tree-filled square just outside the old city walls, or just relax and chat with friends.

## Sa Penya & Botafoch Marina

Sit at any one of the many cafés or bars around the port or in the nearby tiny streets and watch the world go by. The little alleys of Sa Penya, especially around Carrer d'Enmig, are full of shops and stalls selling brightly coloured souvenirs, sunglasses, jewellery and T-shirts. Stop by one of the CD stalls and listen to music all day.

There is plenty going on at just about any time of the day or night. You can take a waterside walk through the port or take a short boat ride to Botafoch Marina and see Dalt Vila floodlit across the water at night.

## TAKING A BREAK

As you wander around the port and the narrow streets of the marina area, there are plenty of bars and restaurants to choose from. During the day look out for the economical *menú del día* (fixed-price menu) in the new part of town.

## Restaurants & cafés

**Bon Profit £** ❶ Paella for €3! Queue up to put your name down for a table as soon as the doors open. Bon Profit serves the best-quality Ibizan food at really low prices. @ Plaça des Parc 5 🕐 13.00–15.00 & 20.00–22.00 Mon–Sat, closed Sun & Dec–Feb

**Out of Time People £** ❷ Join the locals at this little incense-scented hippy café just outside the old city walls. Relax with a mint tea and enjoy

⬥ *The harbour of Ibiza Town*

a salad, veggie burger, fruit or vegetable juice. The café also does tarot readings (book in advance). ⓐ Carrer Jaume 1 (just off Plaça des Parc) ⓣ 971 39 23 21 ⓛ 10.00–01.00 daily

**La Oliva ££** ❸   This typically Mediterranean-style restaurant has a charming rustic interior as well as a seating area outside. It is located in a quaint, narrow street just off Plaça de Vila. ⓐ Carrer Santa Creu ⓣ 971 30 57 52 ⓦ www.ibiza-restaurants.com/laoliva ⓛ 19.30–01.00 daily

**Plaza del Sol ££** ❹   Sit on the open terrace overlooking the city and have coffee at any time – the place buzzes all day and is always busy at mealtimes. ⓐ Plaça del Sol ⓣ 971 18 74 81 ⓦ www.plazadelsolibiza.com ⓛ 19.30–00.30 daily (Apr–Oct)

**El Olivo £££** ❺ The splurge option if you want French cuisine in unique surroundings, including fresh fish and fine seafood. Worth booking in advance. ⓐ Plaça de Vila 8 ❶ 971 30 06 80 ❷ 19.00–01.00 Tues–Sun, closed Mon

**La Raspa £££** ❻ One of Ibiza's top restaurants, La Raspa has fantastic views from the terrace to Dalt Vila. The interior is decorated like a boat and it has its own tank of lobsters. ⓐ Marina Botafoch, local 205 (other side of the harbour) ❶ 971 31 18 10 ❷ 13.00–16.00 & 20.30–24.00 daily

## AFTER DARK

Stroll along the harbour and have a look at the huge luxury cruisers. The clubs of El Divino and Pacha put on big parades to attract attention before they open and these have become part of the nightlife in Ibiza Town. The parades finish in the little streets of Sa Penya, so you'll get a good view anywhere in this area.

### Casino
**Casino de Ibiza** ❼ This is on the road out of town. As well as gaming rooms there is a restaurant, Jackpot (£££), which serves a variety of international dishes as well as pizza. ⓐ Carretera Ibiza-San Antonio ❶ 971 31 33 12 ❿ www.casinoibiza.com ❷ Restaurant 21.00–03.00 daily; Gambling 17.00–06.00 daily

### Bars & clubs
**El Divino** ❽ **& Pacha** ❿ These are two popular clubs across the harbour near the Marina Botafoch. For El Divino, also see page 70.
ⓐ El Divino, Puerto Deportivo ❶ 971 31 83 38
❿ www.eldivino-ibiza.com ❷ 24.00–06.00 daily
ⓐ Pacha, Avinguda 8 d'Agost ❶ 971 31 36 12
❿ www.pacha.com ❷ 24.00–06.00 daily

**Heaven** ❾  Reopening in summer 2010, this well-known club is located near Pacha and El Divino (see opposite). ⓐ Passeig Juan Carlos 1 ❸ 971 31 24 46 ❿ www.heaven-ibiza.com ⏱ 24.00–06.00 daily

**Rock Bar** ⓫  The Rock Bar (and Base Bar next door at No 16 ❸ 971 31 77 86) is the place to see and be seen before the clubs open. ⓐ Carrer Cipriano Garijo 14 ❸ 971 31 01 29 ❿ www.therockbaribiza.com ⏱ 21.00–03.00 daily

🔺 *Take a stroll through the backstreets*

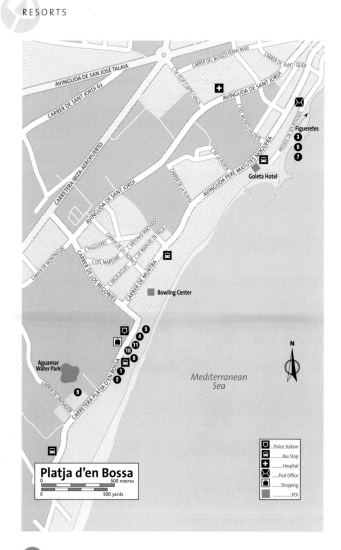

AVINGUDA DE SAN JOSÉ TALAIA

CARRER DEL MÚSICO FERMÍ MARÍ

CARRER DE FONT I QUER

CARRER DE SANT JORDI 62

AVINGUDA DE SANT JORDI

C/DE FELIP CURTOIS VALLS

C/DE INOCENCIO VICENTE

Figueretes

③
⑥
⑦

CARRETERA IBIZA–AEROPUERTO

PASSEIG DE SES PITIÜSES

CARRER DE LA PUNTA

CARRER DE LA PUNTA

AVINGUDA PERE MATUTES NOGUERA

Goleta Hotel

AVINGUDA DE SANT JORDI

C/ ALGUERES

C/ CANTONIO MACHADO

CARRER DE LES ALZINES

C/ DE MANUEL DE FALLA

CARRER DE MONTNEGRE

C/ DEL MARESME

CARRER DE LOS BEGONIES

C/ ANGELAGUES

CARRER DE MURTRA

Bowling Center

N

⑤
④

Aguamar
Water Park

⑩ ⑪
⑧
①
②

⑨

Mediterranean
Sea

CARRETERA PLATJA D'EN BOSSA

CARRETERA D'EN BOSSA

**Platja d'en Bossa**

0 _____ 500 metres

0 _____ 500 yards

| | |
|---|---|
| 🔲 | ...Police Station |
| 🚍 | ...Bus Stop |
| ✚ | ...Hospital |
| ✉ | ...Post Office |
| 🔲 | ...Shopping |
| 🔲 | ...POI |

# Platja d'en Bossa & Figueretes

Platja d'en Bossa is one of the most popular resorts on the island, mainly because it has the longest beach on Ibiza – almost 3 km (2 miles). The gently shelving beach is made of fine sand and backed by a fringe of palm trees. A row of hotels, shops, bars and eating places caters to the many visitors, and all this within a short distance of the airport.

Families like it here because it's very safe for young children, while older ones use the watersports facilities along the beach such as windsurfing and waterskiing. Adults enjoy the nightlife at megaclub Space, or make the short trip into Ibiza Town for shopping and more clubbing.

Between Platja d'en Bossa and Ibiza Town, on the edge of Ibiza Town, is the much smaller resort of Figueretes (the name means 'the little fig trees'). Figueretes has a lovely palm-tree-filled promenade running around the beach, with bars, cafés and restaurants to suit just about anyone. From here you can walk into Ibiza Town in 15 minutes via the town or along the coastal path. Figueretes is one of the popular resorts for gay men.

## BEACHES

**Platja d'en Bossa**'s beach tends to be a little more peaceful at the northern end. The beach at Figueretes is quite narrow, but pleasant, and a water-skiing school can be found here. To the south, **Es Cavallet** is the famous nudist beach, and **Ses Salines** is also popular among party-goers.

### TRANSPORT

Bus No 14 runs between Platja d'en Bossa along to Figueretes and then Ibiza Town (every 20 minutes 07.20–23.40 in summer), see www.ibizabus.com. There are also regular boats from the jetties between these resorts. There are taxi ranks next to both main beaches. The Ibiza Disco Bus blue route (see page 70) runs through here at night. ⓦ www.discobus.es

The salt flats nearby make for interesting walking as the whole area has been declared a nature reserve.

## Beach parties
**Platja d'en Bossa** is famous for its parties. **Bora Bora** (see page 27) has a beach party most afternoons. As does **Space** (see page 27).

## THINGS TO SEE & DO

### Aguamar Water Park
This is the perfect place to spend a day whether or not you have children. There are water-chutes like the Kamikaze and the Black Hole – not for the faint-hearted – with a bar and a restaurant, garden areas and a picnic area. You can get a re-entry pass so you can visit the beach opposite to break up the day and return later.
ⓐ Next to Space (see page 27), off the Carretera Platja d'en Bossa
ⓘ 971 39 67 90  ⏱ 10.00–18.00 daily (Jun–Oct)  ❶ Admission charge

### Bowling Center
This caters for all the family, with a rodeo bull, a bowling alley, mini-golf, pool tables and more.
ⓐ Platja d'en Bossa, Carrer de Murtra 2–4  ☎ 971 30 03 56
⏱ 07.00–02.00 daily

### Cruise
The *Ulises Cat* glass-bottomed boat leaves Figueretes beach and Platja d'en Bossa twice daily for day trips to the beautiful island of Formentera (see page 85).
ⓐ Departs from the front of the Goleta Hotel, Platja d'en Bossa, and the Ibiza Playa Hotel, Figueretes  ❶ Information only: 606 65 48 12
ⓦ www.ulisesibiza.com  ⏱ 09.50 & 11.10 from Figueretes, 10.00 & 11.00 from Platja d'en Bossa, returning at 17.00 & 19.00 daily
❶ No booking required

## TAKING A BREAK

### Restaurants & bars

**Manoa £** **❶** With baguette sandwiches served all day (turkey and pesto or tomato and mozzarella, to name but a few), this laid-back lounge bar has a resident DJ. Choose from more than 50 cocktails in the evening.
ⓐ Carretera Platja d'en Bossa ⓛ 07.00–04.00 daily

**Passion £** **❷** Refresh yourself with fruit juices or refuel after clubbing with home-made burgers and falafel followed by carrot cake.
ⓐ Carretera Platja d'en Bossa ⓣ 971 30 51 30 ⓛ 10.00–24.00 daily

🔺 *Platja d'en Bossa is popular for sailing and windsurfing*

**Chino Taiwan ££** ❸ Tasty Chinese dishes, generous portions and reasonably priced. ⓐ On the main promenade at Figueretes, Passeig de Ses Pitiüses-Figueretes ❶ 971 30 16 19 ⓛ 12.00–24.00 daily

**Moorea ££** ❹ The barbecue keeps going all day cooking fresh fish and meats on the grill. ⓐ Jet Apartments, Carretera Platja d'en Bossa ⓛ 12.00–01.00 daily

**Pago Pago ££** ❺ Right on the beach, this laid-back restaurant serves cocktails and has its own DJ playing chill-out music. Open first thing serving breakfasts, right through to dinner of mussels or pizza. The music starts pumping later as it's a popular pre-party venue. ⓐ Jet Apartments, Carretera Platja d'en Bossa ⓛ 09.00–01.00 daily

**Principe ££** ❻ This place has a shady terrace and specialises in seafood, including lobsters and shellfish fresh from its own tanks. ⓐ Carrer Ramón Muntaner 20, on the beach at Figueretes ❶ 971 30 19 14 ⓛ 12.00–01.00 daily

**Romagna Mia ££** ❼ This Italian restaurant serves pizza, pasta and fresh fish dishes. There is also a very reasonable set menu. ⓐ Carrer Ramón Muntaner 28, on the sea overlooking the promenade at Figueretes ❶ 971 30 59 42 ⓛ 13.00–16.00 & 20.00–24.00 daily

### SHOPPING

Figueretes lacks good shops so most people make the short trip to Ibiza Town for the best places to shop.
**The Hippy Market** A great place to buy arts and crafts, T-shirts, jewellery and souvenirs. ⓐ Carretera Platja d'en Bossa ⓛ 11.00–20.00 Fri
**La Sirena** A gift store and shop close to the Aguamar Water Park with clothes, leather, ceramics and perfume at discount prices. ⓐ Carretera Platja d'en Bossa ❶ 971 30 23 41 ⓛ 09.30–23.30 daily

## AFTER DARK

### Beach parties

Beach parties at the bars along the promenade are always lively and crowded. The most popular spot is the **Bora Bora** ❽ beach bar, where the disco keeps going until 06.00 (❶ 971 30 37 86). **Space** ❾ used to be *the* After Party place until the law changed re: opening times (see page 69). However, it's still regarded as one of the island's best clubs. Check for opening times, which change seasonally. ❶ 971 39 67 93 ⓦ www.space-ibiza.es ❶ 22.00–06.00 Mon–Sat, 16.30–06.00 Sun

### Bars

**Murphy's Irish Bar** ❿ There's live sports on the TV, a band every night, and draught Guinness® at this bar-pub, which caters for children too. ❸ Jet Apartments, Carretera Platja d'en Bossa ⓦ www.murphyspub-ibiza.com ❶ 21.00–06.00 daily

**Top 21** ⓫ Satellite TVs, a cocktail terrace plus a club playing funk, soul and R&B Mon–Thur and Latin American on Fri & Sat. ❸ Jet Apartments, Carretera Platja d'en Bossa ❶ 20.00–05.00 daily

🔺 *Aguamar Water Park*

# Cala Tarida & Cala Vedella

There are some little gems of places in the southwest corner of Ibiza, and these are two of them. Both are small resorts with only a handful of apartments, and no real hotels. A couple of well-situated eating places look out over the beach and the sea, and there are several shops to provide your basic provisions in the little town above the beach.

## BEACHES

**Cala Tarida** doesn't have a huge beach – it's made up of three small sections of sand with a few rocks at each end where, if the beach becomes too crowded, you can grab a sunbathing spot – but it shelves gently into the sea so is great for young children. It also has excellent facilities.

At **Cala Vedella**, the beach is wide and sandy, and although it is smaller and can get crowded, it is in a very special location. At one end the holiday complex resembles a Spanish village with terracotta chimneys. In the middle the shops and restaurants are right on the beach. The cove is protected from the wind so it has become a popular mooring for small yachts and boats.

There are several other more secluded beaches along this coast, such as **Cala Moli** and **Cala d'en Reial**, some accessible by car, others only by hiring a boat.

## THINGS TO SEE & DO

### Excursions
**Cala d'Hort** is not far away at the end of a very steep, winding road, and is definitely worth making the effort to visit, although it can only be reached by taxi or private car. The beach is small and sandy with one little shop and a couple of excellent beachside restaurants, and that's it. It's a blissful place, reminiscent of a tropical island beach with its palm and fig trees, which is probably why it was chosen as a location for the

film of the Rodgers and Hammerstein musical *South Pacific*. Out to sea is the small, steep-cliffed island of Es Vedrà – said to have mystical powers.

Here, you might see a flock of the very rare Eleonora's falcons that live in the nearby cliffs. There are only about 500 of these small birds of prey in the whole of the Mediterranean, and they're the only birds of prey that live in groups. If you can, look in the early evening sky to watch them flocking and catching insects.

Cala d'Hort is very busy, especially at weekends, and car-parking space is limited. You can drive down to the end of the road, although it can be a bit of a tight squeeze so it's better to park further up the hill.

## Watersports

Both Cala Tarida and Cala Vedella have diving centres.

**Cala Tarida** On the beach at Cala Tarida, a little hut offers waterskiing, pedaloes and a banana boat. The resort even has a glass-bottomed boat.

◗ *Soaking up the sun at Cala Tarida*

**Orca Sub Diving Centre** There are English-speaking PADI (Professional Association of Diving Instructors) instructors here.
ⓐ Insotel Club, Tarida beach ⓣ 971 80 63 07 ⓦ www.orcasub.net
**Cala Vedella** The dive centre at Cala Vedella, Big Blue Dive, is just behind the beach near the main car park.
ⓣ 650 76 92 96 ⓦ www.bigbluedive.net

## TAKING A BREAK

### Restaurants
**Cala d'Hort ££** You feel like an extra in *South Pacific* in this delightful beach restaurant serving delicious fresh fish, paella and crème caramels with relaxed service. ⓐ Right-hand side of the beach, Cala d'Hort
ⓣ 971 93 50 36 ⓛ 13.00–22.00 daily ⓘ No credit cards

**Can Jaume ££** At one end of the beach, Can Jaume serves a good selection of pasta and seafood. ⓐ Platja Cala Vedella, near the main car park ⓣ 971 80 84 88 ⓛ 12.00–24.00 Tues–Sun, closed Mon

🔺 *A cove at Cala Tarida*

## SHOPPING

There are several small supermarkets and souvenir shops along the main street in Cala Tarida such as the **Supermarket Cala Sol** (good for spirits and beach gear), **Supermarket Stop II** and the **Cala Tarida Supermarket**. In Cala d'Hort, the **Boutique Azibi** is a real beach shop a short walk back from the beach selling smart sarongs and a range of beachwear. In Cala Vedella, there are a couple of small shops in the holiday village, and the hippy beachfront shop **Alquimia** sells sarongs, kaftans, T-shirts and hammocks. **Cala Vedella Supermarket** is on the road to Cala Moli.

**El Carmen ££** This restaurant overlooks the middle of the beach, with views out to the island. It serves a typical Spanish menu: fish, paella, pizza and meat dishes. **ⓐ** Overlooking the middle of the beach, Cala d'Hort **ⓣ** 971 18 74 49 **ⓛ** 12.30–23.30 daily (Mar–Oct)

**C'as Mila ££** Right above the beach, C'as Mila serves casual lunches and slightly smarter romantic evening meals. Choose your lobster or shellfish from the tanks or go for the catch of the day. There are plenty of meat dishes too. Sometimes there is live music on Saturday night. **ⓐ** Above the beach at Cala Tarida **ⓣ** 971 80 61 93 **ⓦ** www.restaurantecasmila.com **ⓛ** 13.00–16.00 & 19.00–24.00 daily (May–Oct); lunch & dinner Sat, lunch Sun (Nov–Apr)

**Maria Luisa ££** Overlooking the beach, this family-run restaurant is the perfect place to enjoy lobster or fresh fish. **ⓐ** Cala Vedella **ⓣ** 971 80 80 12 **ⓛ** 12.00–24.00 daily

**Ses Eufabies ££** Perched on top of a small rock, this smart, tiny restaurant sits in the middle of the beach overlooking the sun-loungers. Good for paella and fresh fish dishes on its charming terrace. **ⓐ** Cala Tarida **ⓣ** 971 80 63 28 **ⓦ** www.eufabies.com **ⓛ** 12.00–16.30 & 19.00–23.30 daily

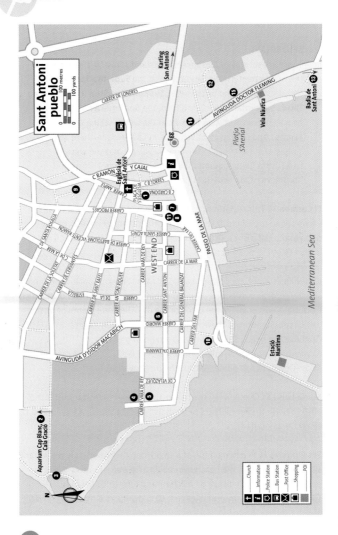

Sant Antoni
pueblo

0    100 metres
0    100 yards

Karting
San Antonio

CARRER DE LONDRES

AVINGUDA DOCTOR FLEMING

Badia de
Sant Antoni

Vela Nàutica

Platja
S'Arenal

Egg

C RAMON Y CAJAL

Església de
Sant Antoni

C B TORRES

CARRER AMPLE

PLAÇA DE
S'ESGLÉSIA

C CARDONA

CARRER PROGRÉS

CARRER SANTA AGNÈS

CARRER DE BARTOLOME VICENTE RAMÓN

CARRER DE SANTA ROSALIA

CARRER DE LA MAR

C DE LA MAR

CARRER DE CERVANTES

CARRER DE LA SOLETAT

ESTRELLA

CARRER DE SANT RAFEL

CARRER ANTONI ROQUER

CARRER DE LA

CARRER VARA DE REY

WEST END

CARRER DE LA MAR

PASSEIG DE LA MAR

CARRERS DE MAR

CARRER SANT ANTONI

CARRER DEL GENERAL BALANZAT

CARRER MADRID

CARRER DES FAR

CARRER D'ALEMANYA

AVINGUDA D'ISIDOR MACABICH

C DE VELÁZQUEZ

CARRER VARA DE REY

Estació
Marítima

Aquarium Cap Blanc
Cala Gració

Mediterranean Sea

N

Church
Information
Police Station
Bus Station
Post Office
Shopping
POI

# Sant Antoni pueblo (San Antonio town)

Ibiza's second town (more commonly known as San Antonio or San An) is popular with clubbers, although the party atmosphere does not start until late in the evening. The town is home to Ibiza's famous sunset strip, where all ages gather to watch the sun go down at one of the many cafés and bars.

It's hard to believe that this was a tiny fishing village about 40 years ago, blessed with a large natural harbour. Tourism came, and the village grew, then the club scene arrived, and the place grew again.

The harbour is one of the town's focal points for an evening stroll. Here, you can book a boat trip or ferry to any one of the smaller beaches in the area, organise diving, speedboats or paragliding. The beach is quite small and very crowded in summer, but there are a few beachfront bars where you can watch the world go by. At the eastern end in the middle of a roundabout is the 'egg' statue celebrating Christopher Columbus, who possibly came from Ibiza although several other places claim him too. When he was trying to raise money to find a route through to the Far East, Columbus was told the route was impossible. He took an egg and asked people if they also thought it was impossible to stand the egg upright. When they said that it was, he gently cracked the base to flatten it, and stood it on end. 'Nothing is impossible,' he said.

## BEACHES

The beach in the centre of San Antonio is small, but it does have the basic facilities. Unfortunately, it's right by the road. You can walk north, and over to the far side of the headland for another small beach at Caló des Moro, or take a bus or ferry to one of the many nearby beaches in San Antonio Bay. The nearest beach in San Antonio Bay is only a 10- to 15-minute walk along the promenade. Small boats leave from the port of San Antonio throughout the day for Cala Bassa – a small bay backed by pine trees so there is plenty of shade. It's a popular place, with waterskis and lilos for hire. There are cafés and restaurants behind the beach.

## THINGS TO SEE & DO

### Aquarium Cap Blanc

This natural cave with its shallow waters was once used by fishermen to protect their catch. It is now an illuminated grotto and aquarium showing off the local sea creatures – great for children. There's also a chance to swim outside and have a drink on the bar terrace.

ⓐ Carretera de Cala Gració (in front of Tanit Hotel), Cala Gració
ⓘ 663 94 54 75 🕐 09.00–22.00 daily ❶ Admission charge

### Cycling

Hire a bike from the tourist office for free (deposit of €50 required) and cycle around to San Antonio Bay. If you're feeling a little more energetic, bike all the way to Cala Comte on the new bike route No 1. It's classed as an easy green ride of 13 km (8 miles).

ⓦ www.ibizacicloturismo.com

### Karting San Antonio

There's a track and pizzeria on the edge of town, on the road to Sant Rafel.

ⓐ Carretera Ibiza-Sant Antoni Km 14 ⓘ 971 34 38 05
ⓦ www.kartingsanantonio.com 🕐 10.00–24.00 daily

### Parasailing

Fly 200 m (656 ft) over the bay for a bird's-eye view of San Antonio and the surrounding area.

ⓐ Jimmy's Parasailing at Hotel Es Pins Sailing School and San Antonio Harbour ⓘ 606 82 25 02 ⓦ www.digitalibiza.com/parasailing
🕐 Mid-Apr–mid-Oct

### Powerboating

Start the adrenalin pumping on *Wicked* – the fastest powerboat in Ibiza – as it zooms around the bay.

ⓐ At the port near the Egg ⓘ 669 32 55 11
ⓦ www.wickedparasailing.com 🕐 May–Oct

## Promenade by night

A great way to work up an appetite, whether for food or a night on the town, is to go for a stroll along the Passeig Marítim promenade. The seafront promenade has recently been extended from the Hawaii hotel in San Antonio Bay right up to the Aquarium at Cala Gració, taking in the Sunset Strip and its bars.

## Sailing & windsurfing

At Platja s'Arenal, Julian and his daughter Oren are qualified English-speaking instructors who also rent out boats, windsurfers and kayaks.
ⓐ Platja s'Arenal, Avinguda Doctor Fleming ❶ 971 34 65 35
🕐 08.00–22.00 daily

## Scenic train trip

Kids and adults will love the two-hour ride on this miniature train taking you up to El Mirador, one of the highest peaks on the island.
ⓐ San Antonio bus station ❶ 636 99 82 95 (Ignacio) 🕐 Departures 11.00, 13.00 & 16.00 ❶ Admission charge

🔺 *The daily ritual of watching the sun go down*

## EXCURSIONS
### Cala Gració

At the northern end of San Antonio, and accessible from there by car, boat or on foot on the promenade, Cala Gració is small but almost a resort in itself. There is a small beach, the Aquarium and several bars, cafés and restaurants.

### Formentera Island

Take the boat to Formentera (see page 85) for the day and visit this charming island.

🕒 Departs San Antonio on the promenade near the Egg 10.30 and leaves Formentera 17.00 ☎ 971 34 34 71 🌐 www.crucerosportmany.com

### Glass-bottomed boat trip

Take a three-hour boat trip around the bay to Es Vedrà (see page 83), taking in the bays of Cala Tarida, Cala Vedella and others. This is a good chance to see the marine life and something of Es Vedrà.

🅐 Departs from the waterfront promenade near the Egg ☎ 971 34 34 71 🌐 www.crucerosportmany.com 🕒 Enquire about days & times

### SHOPPING

There are plenty of souvenir shops along the pedestrian streets in the West End around Carrer Progrés. **Casa Alfonso**, the first supermarket on Ibiza, stocks local and British foods and has an off-licence (🅐 Near the junction of Carrers Ample and Sant Antoni at Carrer Progrés 8 ☎ 971 34 05 10 🕒 09.00–22.30 Mon–Sat, closed Sun).

Further along Carrer Sant Antoni is the **May Shopping Centre/department store** arranged on four floors. It sells sports goods, clothes, souvenirs galore, brand names, alcohol and cigarettes (🅐 Carrer Sant Antoni 13 ☎ 971 34 00 86 🕒 09.30–22.00 Mon–Sat, 10.00–14.00, 17.00–21.00 Sun).

## TAKING A BREAK

### Restaurants & cafés

There are several waterside café-bars along what is commonly known as the Sunset Strip and a little further on at Caló des Moro where people gather for the daily ritual of watching the sunset. All of the café-bars play ambient trance music to chill out to. Later in the evening the café-bars act as pre-party places for the larger clubs.

**Café Babel £** ❶ Stop by for teas, fresh juices and wines in this tiny little café, and relax while you smell the incense sticks and listen to neo-soul music. ⓐ Plaça de s'Església 2 ❶ 971 80 40 50 ❻ 12.00–02.00 daily ❶ Wi-fi available

**Kasbah £** ❷ The menu is geared towards an international market with a fusion of flavours. An added bonus is that you can also watch the sunset here from one of the driftwood tables and chairs. ⓐ Carrer Soledad 68, Caló des Moro ❶ 971 34 83 64 ❻ 12.00–24.00 daily

**Sun Sea Bar £** ❸ The resident DJs play classic ambient chill-out and soulful house music at this sunset bar. Order your drink from the boat-shaped bar and choose your seafood straight from the tank. ⓐ Carrer de Cervantes 50, Caló des Moro ❶ 971 80 37 78 ⓦ www.sunseabar-ibiza.com ❻ 10.00–01.00 daily (Apr–Oct)

**Café Mambo ££** ❹ During the day, this a good place to go for something to eat and to hang out on the beach in front. Later, at sunset, it fills up with a cocktail-drinking crowd. ⓐ Carrer Vara de Rey 40 ❶ 971 34 66 38 ⓦ www.cafemamboibiza.com ❻ 11.00–04.00 daily

**Café del Mar ££** ❺ This is still the sunset bar to go to, with a resident DJ. Once the sun sets, stay to watch the fire-eater on the rocks. This is the only sunset bar that doesn't serve food. ⓐ Carrer Vara de Rey 27 ❻ 17.00–01.00 daily

**The Curry Club ££** ❻  Choose from a range of Indian dishes. This is a tranquil place, away from the mayhem of the West End, where you can eat in the beautifully designed restaurant or in its tropical gardens.
ⓐ Corner of Carrers Sant Antoni & Madrid ❶ 971 34 36 04
🕑 19.00–24.00 daily (Apr–Oct)

**Mei Ling ££** ❼  A big, popular Chinese restaurant on the main promenade near the fountain. All the usual dishes, like sweet-and-sour pork and spicy prawns, but you can also just order chips and curry sauce.
ⓐ Carrer Ample 1 ❶ 971 34 34 14 🕑 17.00–01.00 daily (July & Aug);
17.00–24.00 daily (Sept–June)

**El Rincon de Pepe ££** ❽  The cuisine here is Spanish with tapas and steak. ⓐ Carrer Sant Mateu 6 ❶ 971 34 06 97 🆆 www.rincondepepe.net
🕑 11.00–01.00 daily

**Tijuana ££** ❾  A Tex-Mex restaurant where dishes like burritos and barbecue ribs are served with margaritas and Mexican beers. Live mariachi music every Friday. ⓐ Carrer Ramón y Cajal 23 ❶ 971 34 24 73
🆆 www.tijuanatexmex.com 🕑 18.30–01.00 daily (Apr–Oct); 19.30–01.00 Thur–Sat (Nov–Mar)

🔺 *Café Mambo is a very popular sunset bar*

**El Yate ££ ⑩** This restaurant serves fresh fish dishes and is one of the best places in town for tapas such as anchovies, *chorizo* and tortilla. Located at the end of the port by the sea, just before the promenade to the sunset bars. ⓐ Passeig Maritim de Sant Antoni ① 971 34 60 55 ① 13.00–16.00, 20.30–24.00 daily ① Wi-fi available

## AFTER DARK

The West End, as the main area of San Antonio is known, is filled with drinking places and geared towards young clubbers. Most of the bars and pubs stay open until the early hours. Some of the more popular places include Murphy's Irish Pub, Koppas, Joe Spoon's and Cheers. Along the beachfront, the main bars are Bar M and Itaca.

### Bars & clubs

**Breezes ⑪** Famous for the Dead Man Walking 4-litre cocktail based on absinthe (only three people have ever managed to drink it all) and the Big Jug o'Love, this pub-bar also serves shots and draught beers. ⓐ Carrer Sant Antoni 5 ⓦ www.digitalibiza.com/breezes ① 17.00–03.00 daily

**Eden ⑫ & Es Paradis ⑮** These are the big clubs here (see page 73). ⓐ Just off the Avinguda Dr Fleming on Carrer Salvador Espriu

**Ibiza Rocks ⑬** A combined hotel and music venue which attracts the hippest bands to its Tuesday-night gigs. ⓐ Carrer Cervantes 27 ⓦ www.ibizarocks.com

**Plastik ⑭** There are club days and nights and pre-club parties here. ⓐ Avinguda Dr Fleming, near the Egg ⓦ www.plastikibiza.com ① 22.00–04.00 daily

See pages 68–75 for more information on Ibiza's club scene and evening entertainment options.

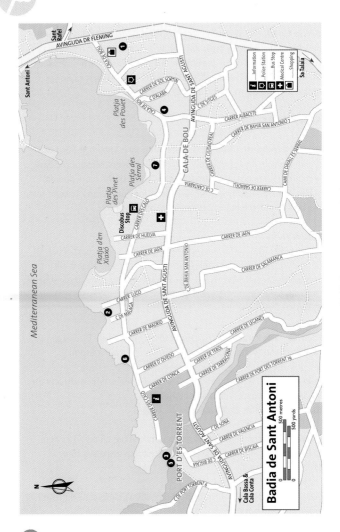

# Badia de Sant Antoni (San Antonio Bay)

The area generally referred to as San Antonio Bay runs south from the town of Sant Antoni (San Antonio). This is a big bay, and there are plenty of small resorts and beaches in both directions from the main town. The first main area you come to is called Cala de Bou and is on the far side of San Antonio's harbour, which these days is more or less a continuation of the main town. From the edge of San Antonio right along the bay, the main street stretches for several kilometres and is lined with bars, cafés, shops and restaurants.

**Cala de Bou** has several small beaches, so the crowds tend to be dispersed among them. They're all within walking distance of San Antonio if you want a change of scene, though of course the hotels have all the facilities you might want – and remember you don't have to be a resident to enjoy using them.

Further around the Bay is **Port d'es Torrent**, a tiny old village that has become a favourite tourist centre. A little further on is the incredibly popular beach of **Cala Bassa** in a lovely bay backed by cliffs. From the top of the cliffs there's a terrific view back to San Antonio, from where regular boat trips bring plenty of day visitors.

## THINGS TO SEE & DO

### Cycling
**From Cala de Bou to Cala Bassa** There is an easy route from San Antonio Bay to the closest beach, Cala Bassa. If you have enough time, continue west to Cala Conta, enjoying the landscape and splendid views.
Ⓦ www.ibizacicloturismo.com

### Walking
Take a stroll around the boat-filled bay. The waterfront promenade is lined with cafés, shops and restaurants and there is always plenty of activity. The uninhabited island of Conillera, with its lighthouse,

dominates the view. It is possible to take a small boat there and walk among the pine trees and wild flowers.

## EXCURSIONS
### Climb Sa Talaia
If you're feeling energetic, head south to the village of Sant Josep, from where it's about a two-hour walk to the top of Ibiza's highest peak, Sa Talaia (475 m/1,560 ft), and back.

### Sant Rafel
This village on the road to Ibiza Town has good views of Dalt Vila from the plaza by the church and is the main spot for ceramic production.

## TAKING A BREAK

### Restaurants
The bay area is very well off for eating places, whether you want Thai, Spanish, English or Italian.

**Casa Thai £** ❶ Cheap and cheerful Thai restaurant on the main road with an excellently priced menu of spring rolls and Thai green curry. It also offers a takeaway service. 🅐 Avinguda Dr Fleming 34 ☎ 971 34 40 38 🕒 13.00–23.30 daily

**Kumharas £** ❷ Kumharas opens for breakfast and lunch with juices, teas and salads before serving an Asian–Mediterranean fusion menu in the evening. You can lounge around on the leather floor cushions, or sit by

the bar. This is also an ideal place for a quiet drink at sunset when you may also find fire-eaters, jugglers, a few hippy stalls and a range of musical performers providing entertainment. ⓐ On the beach at the end of Carrer Lugo ⓣ 971 80 57 40 ⓦ www.kumharas.org ⓛ 12.00–04.00 daily

**Es Turrent £** ❸ A tiny little beachfront bar at the Port d'es Torrent. After 18.00 it's drinks only, but on Sundays you can fill up on mixed grill at the barbecue from 20.30. ⓐ On the beach at Platja de Port d'es Torrent

**Casita ££** ❹ A British restaurant serving favourites including shepherd's pie, chilli con carne and pasta bake. Set under a huge awning around a pine tree. ⓐ Avinguda Cala de Bou 19, Cala de Bou ⓣ 971 34 16 08 ⓦ www.ibizacasita.com ⓛ 18.00–23.00 daily

**Es Virot ££** ❺ Set just off the beach, you can hear the waves break as you sip your sangría. Good for pasta, pizza and salads. ⓐ Carrer Biscala, Platja de Port d'es Torrent ⓣ 971 80 34 66 ⓛ 12.00–24.00 daily

**Can Pujol £££** ❻ A contender for best fish restaurant on the island, Can Pujol is right on the beach. Pick your seafood from the tank or try oysters, stone bass or angler fish. If you fancy trying an Ibizan speciality, pick the *espardenyes* (sea cucumbers). ⓐ Old Port d'es Torrent road, on the beach ⓣ 971 34 14 07 ⓛ 13.00–16.00 & 19.30–23.30 Thur–Tues, closed Wed

## AFTER DARK

### Clubs
If you're looking for clubs, then San Antonio is the place to go. The bay is full of pubs with live TV and late-night amusement bars and everything from children's go-karts to bucking broncos and bungee swings.

**Summum** ❼ Resident and guest DJs play dance music amid classical decor. ⓐ Carretera de Port d'es Torrent ⓛ Thur–Sun 22.00–06.30, closed Mon–Wed

# Portinatx & Port de Sant Miquel

These two resorts on the rugged northwest coast of Ibiza are very different. Portinatx (pronounced 'port-ee-natch') is a pretty family resort, the slightly larger of the two and the main resort on this coast. It has several beaches, lovely clear waters and plenty of eating places and bars. Portinatx's main town is higher up the hill, with the port at the bottom of the road. For the more energetic, there are some tough cliff walks, promising spectacular views and unspoiled pine forest scenery.

By contrast, the main town of Sant Miquel is a short way inland, and is hardly affected by tourism, although it does offer a wider range of shopping other than the supermarkets and souvenir shops. It is a small place built up around a lovely bay, and is more correctly known as Port de Sant Miquel.

*Portinatx has clear waters and quiet coves as well as watersports and walks*

## BEACHES

Portinatx has three main beaches, of which the quietest is the last one you come to at the bottom of the hill on the main road. Fishing boats line up on the shore, while on the other side of the car park the rocky crags are great for exploring. **S'Arenal Gros** is the main beach with the smaller **S'Arenal Petit** right next door almost joined together. Both are below the main town. There are also some quiet coves, such as **Cala Xarraca**, **Cala d'en Serra** and **S'illot**, which can also be reached by boat.

Sant Miquel's one main beach is always busy, but if you want somewhere quieter and you have a car, drive northwest to nearby **Cala de Benirràs**.

## THINGS TO SEE & DO

### Can Marça Caves

These illuminated caves are the largest on the island. Located high above Sant Miquel (it's a very steep, long climb up and further than the signposted 500 m/550 yds), the 30-minute guided visits are timed, but the view from the café is worth the wait. ❶ 971 33 47 76 ❷ 10.30–19.30 daily ❶ Admission charge

### Dancing in Sant Miquel village

Traditional dancing takes place outside the church in this inland village every Thursday at about 18.00. There's also an arts and crafts market on Thursdays from 18.00 to 22.00.

### Excursions

Portinatx and Sant Miquel are linked by ferry and by road train. You can also take a boat trip from either resort to one of the quieter bays along the coast. Keen walkers might like to tackle the old bridle path, which is 11 km (7 miles) long and leads to the inland village of Sant Joan. Take plenty of water with you to drink along the way, and do not attempt the walk in the full heat of the day – some parts are very steep.

## Watersports

Try scuba-diving at Portinatx with **Subfari** (ⓐ Puerto de Portinatx
ⓣ 689 25 30 01 ⓦ www.subfari.es). Windsurfing, boats, pedaloes and
banana boats are available at both beaches. Waterskiing is also popular at
Sant Miquel, and there's a glass-bottomed boat that tours the bay.

## TAKING A BREAK

### Restaurants & bars

**Delboy's English Bar £** Hard to miss, with the yellow Reliant Robin parked
outside, Delboy's serves up Sunday roasts and other British favourites,
with evening entertainment from live sports coverage to karaoke. Bring
your laptop and use the wi-fi internet. ⓐ Next to the coach park above
the main beach of S'Arenal Gros, Portinatx ⓛ 10.00–02.00 daily
ⓦ www.delboys-bar.co.uk

**El Puerto £** Serves soups, meat dishes, pizza, fresh fish, lobster and
paella. Right on the small beach accessed by steps or via the quayside
from the car park. ⓐ Puerto de Portinatx ⓣ 971 32 07 76 ⓛ 11.30–16.00 &
19.00–23.00 daily, closed Mon eve

### SHOPPING

The beach resort of Cala Sant Miquel has the usual row of
souvenir and beach shops. All the 'real' shops are found in the
inland village of Sant Miquel, which also has a weekly arts and
crafts market on Thursdays from 18.00.

Portinatx has a good cluster of bars, restaurants and shops in the
town itself. For a good choice of drinks there's the **Boozy Buys** off-
licence and money exchange, which sells some of the cheapest
alcohol on the island, and there are a couple of clothes boutiques.
In the central area by the taxis, you'll find **Rincón Verde**, selling a
good range of local ceramics and paintings. Portinatx's **Hippy
Market** is on Sundays at 18.00.

**S'Arena ££** Up in the main town, this recommended restaurant overlooks the resort and specialises in paella, fresh fish and grills. ⓐ Just past Rincón Verde going down to the port, Portinatx ⓣ 971 32 05 15 ⓛ 12.00–16.00 & 19.00–23.00 daily

**Cas Mallorqui ££** Enjoy fresh fish, paella and authentic local cuisine from this popular restaurant overlooking the harbour. Access by steep steps or via the quayside from the car park. ⓐ Puerto de Portinatx ⓣ 971 32 05 05 ⓛ 13.00–16.30 & 19.00–22.00 daily

**Port Balanzat ££** Some say this is the best fish place on the island, with local specialities such as paella, fish stew, fish soup, squid fried in batter and pizza. ⓐ On Sant Miquel beach, to the left of the beach as you approach it, Port de Sant Miquel ⓣ 971 33 45 27 ⓛ 13.00–16.00 & 20.00–23.30 daily

**Restaurante Jardín del Mar ££** This simple café-restaurant sits above the sea and even has its own mini-golf course. Choose from pizza, fresh fish and great salads. ⓐ In a prime spot overlooking the main beach at Portinatx ⓣ 971 32 07 52 ⓛ 12.00–16.00 & 19.00–24.00 daily

**Eden Restaurant £££** Enjoy the stunning views from this clifftop hotel, which complement the exceptional Mediterranean menu. Arrive early and watch the sunset with a cocktail. Vegetarians are well catered for. ⓐ Hotel Hacienda Na Xamena, near Port de Sant Miquel ⓣ 971 33 45 00 ⓦ www.hotelhacienda-ibiza.com ⓛ 13.00–16.00 & 20.00–23.00 daily

## AFTER DARK

### Bar
**Vicente's Bar** An English bar with live sports coverage and nightly entertainment. ⓐ Next to the coach park above the main beach of S'Arenal Gros, Portinatx ⓛ 20.00–03.00 daily

# Cala Sant Vicent

As you approach the resort of Cala Sant Vicent along twisting hill roads, you will drive through some of the pine forests that caused the Greeks to call Ibiza and Formentera the 'pine islands'. Cala Sant Vicent is a tiny place but well worth a day out even if only to enjoy its clean beach and peaceful location. You can also try the excellent eating places overlooking the beach where some of the freshest fish on the island is served.

A few years ago there was nothing here except for the pretty inlet with a long and gently curving sandy beach. However, a string of apartments and hotels has been developed behind the little promenade, and there are also enough shops and cheaper eating places here now to satisfy most visitors. With its palm-fringed pedestrian promenade and shallow waters, the resort is an especially good place to bring children. There's very little to do at Cala Sant Vicent other than eat and go to the beach, but you can enjoy watersports, volleyball and even a mini-golf course. There are some good walks, too, for the more energetically minded. You may come across Sant Vicent Church and traditional old farmhouses dotted about the hillsides on your travels.

## BEACHES

**Sant Vicent's** beach lies in a beautiful cove. It is clean and well maintained with sun-loungers and umbrellas for hire as well as beach showers. There are other good beaches you can get to by boat or road at **Es Figueral** and **Pou des Lleó** to the south. The beach at Es Figueral is narrow and sandy and has good watersports facilities and beach amenities. Pou des Lléo is quiet with basic facilities, although it's popular with Ibizans on a warm summer's night.

If you like to strip off on the beach, you might be tempted by Ibiza's second official nudist beach (the other is at Es Cavallet) south of Cala Sant Vicent at **Aiguës Blanques**. It's only a narrow stretch of sand, though, and you'd be better advised to try to find yourself a private secluded cove.

○ The bay at Cala Sant Vicent

## THINGS TO SEE & DO

### Mini-train

A road train winds its way through the bends in the hill roads and takes you to the nearby resorts of Portinatx and Sant Miquel (see page 44).

**t** 971 33 97 72 **!** Admission charge

### Watersports

Pedaloes and boats can be hired, and there is a diving school, Mundo Azul.

**t** 971 32 01 66/689 45 31 52 **w** www.divingcenter-ibiza.com

## EXCURSIONS

### Es Cuieram

Walk to the cave of Es Cuieram, an important archaeological find on Ibiza. It was once a shrine to Tanit, the Carthaginian goddess, and when it was rediscovered in 1907 it was full of gold medallions and terracotta figures. Many of the finds are on display in the Museu Arqueològic de Dalt Vila (see page 17), so there's not much to see in the cave now. There are occasional guided tours from Sant Vicent village, for which the tourist office should be able to give you details.

**a** Between Sant Vicent and Cala Sant Vicent **t** 971 31 09 00 **l** For visiting times call the tourist office

### Punta Grossa

Walk north to the cliffs of Punta Grossa, with wonderful views back to Cala Sant Vicent and along the coast to the north. Take care when walking, as the cliffs are steep and unprotected.

### Sant Carles de Peralta

If you've hired a car, take the road towards Santa Eulària and make a stop in the pretty little inland village of Sant Carles de Peralta (see page 78). You'll understand why the hippies of the 1960s made it one of their main bases on Ibiza.

## Tagomago

Take a boat to the private offshore island of Tagomago, which is to the south of Cala Sant Vicent. This is a good place for a picnic and it has two tiny beaches. However, it's better suited for swimming and fishing than sunbathing.

## TAKING A BREAK

### Restaurants

**Es Gorch £** Serves both meals and drinks, including cocktails and, during the day, its own fresh orange 'vitamin drink'. ⓐ At the back of the beach, to the right as you approach it ⓣ 971 32 01 44 ⓛ 10.00–19.00 Tues–Sun (May–Oct), closed Mon (Sept–July)

**Pizzeria Ole £** With a pizza menu and all the typical favourites of steak, salads and sandwiches, you can enjoy a drink before checking your emails on one of the restaurant's three computers. ⓐ Edificio Las Adelfas ⓣ 971 32 01 37 ⓛ 12.00–24.00 daily

**Es Caló ££** The fish dishes here are exceptional, with Mediterranean cuisine also on offer. ⓐ Right on the seafront ⓣ 971 32 01 40 ⓛ 10.00–24.00 daily (closed Dec–mid-Feb)

**Can Gat ££** The original 'fish house' of Cala Sant Vicent. ⓐ On the beach to the far left ⓣ 971 32 01 23 ⓛ 13.00–16.30 & 20.00–23.00 daily, closed Mon eve

### SHOPPING

**Can Gat** along the waterfront is a very well-stocked souvenir and general shop, with plenty of newspapers and magazines, and a wide range of paperbacks, guidebooks, maps and postcards. For food and other provisions, there's a **Spar** supermarket on the left as you enter Cala Sant Vicent, behind the row of beachfront hotels and opposite Pizzeria Ole.

◓ *The quiet beach at Es Canar*

# Es Canar

It wasn't so long ago that there was nothing at Es Canar but a lovely beach. Then in 1964 enterprising British owners built the Panorama Hotel and a resort was born. It has developed as more of a family resort than some others because of the lovely safe beach and the fact that it's a fair way from the nightlife in Ibiza Town and San Antonio. The resort also feels brighter than some as it's one of the handful of resorts not based in a cove.

The fact that Es Canar is quiet does not mean that there's nothing to do. There are plenty of bars and restaurants; even on a fortnight's visit you could eat and drink somewhere different every night. There are a handful of English pubs, most with entertainment, and plenty of shops. Es Canar is also home to one of the biggest Hippy Markets on the island (🕐 Wed from 10.00).

## BEACHES

Es Canar has a lovely crescent-shaped sandy beach with lots of facilities and restaurants, which is why it's so popular with families. A short walk away is the quieter – and just as attractive but smaller – **Cala Nova**, located near the campsite. There's also a nice beach at **S'Argamassa**, backed by pine trees and with all the basic amenities, plus pedaloes for hire and a handy restaurant.

## THINGS TO SEE & DO

### Cycling

There are two cycle hire shops in town. Why not spend a day exploring the pretty scenery to the north of the island? The land around here is pretty flat, making it ideal for cyclists.

🅐 Kandani, Carretera Santa Eulària-Es Canar 📞 971 33 92 64

🕐 09.00–13.30 & 16.30–21.00 Mon–Fri, 09.00–13.30 Sat, closed Sun

## Excursions

From Es Canar, by heading towards Punta Arabi and then continuing, you can walk the 6 km (3¾ miles) south along the coast all the way to Santa Eulària. You'll see coves and quiet beaches, and there are plenty of places to stop for a drink and a rest. You can always get the bus or a taxi back if you're feeling tired. An hour's walk in the other direction leads to Cala Llenya, through pinewoods, and to another sandy beach.

## Ferry

The ferry departs several times a day for different areas. Take the boat southwest along the coast to Santa Eulària or Cala Llonga, spend some time shopping in Ibiza Town, or relaxing over on Formentera island.
Ⓦ www.ferrysantaeulalia.com

## Glass-bottomed boat trips

Take a look at life under the sea and at a shipwreck off the coast of Es Canar in one of the regular tours from the harbour.
Ⓦ www.ferrysantaeulalia.com

## The Hippy Market

This is one of the biggest markets on the island. Follow the signs from Es Canar and it's just a short walk to the many dozens of stalls selling clothes, jewellery, paintings, carvings and leather. There's a self-service

### SHOPPING

There is a wide selection of shops in the resort. The **Groch** perfume shop is on your right as you enter Es Canar (ⓐ Avinguda d'Es Canar), with a huge stock of well-known names, and jewellery too. **Juma** has a good range of Lladró and Majorica pearls, and also sells crystal, watches and other more expensive items (ⓐ On your right on the street that leaves Es Canar towards Punta Arabi, Plaça d'Es Canar). Don't miss the Hippy Market on Wednesday.

● *Es Canar harbour*

restaurant in the centre of the market, and all sorts of performers ready to provide some impromptu entertainment. Watch your wallets and purses at the Hippy Market. Theft is not a major problem on Ibiza, but it is a favourite place for pickpockets due to the jostling crowds, especially at the height of the season.

ⓐ Punta Arabi ● 10.00–19.00 Wed (May–Oct)

## Watersports

Try watersports at Cesar's Water Sports in S'Argamassa. There is a windsurfing and sailing school, plus parascending, boat hire and lots of other facilities.

ⓐ Cesar's Water Sports, S'Argamassa beach ❶ 971 33 09 19/670 62 99 61
ⓦ www.ibiza-spotlight.com/cesars ● 10.00–19.00 daily (May–Oct)

## TAKING A BREAK

### Restaurants & bars

**Rockerfellers £** This snack-bar and pub has a pool out the back and a computer for internet use. **ⓐ** Avinguda Punta Arabi **ⓣ** 971 33 98 44 **ⓛ** 11.00–24.00 daily

**Zodiac £** Sit around the pool and enjoy simple snacks as well as full meals like steak and spaghetti, and a great choice of puddings. In the evening, there's a varied entertainment programme. **ⓐ** On the left of the road that leads to Punta Arabi, near the ferry terminus, Avinguda Punta Arabi **ⓣ** 971 33 08 22 **ⓛ** 09.00–16.00, 18.00–23.00 daily

**Jacaranda £–££** Right by the ferry, this little place is bright and clean and serves great-value breakfasts, snacks, teas and cocktails. **ⓐ** Avinguda Punta Arabi, next to the ferry **ⓣ** 971 18 61 28 **ⓛ** 09.00–02.00 daily

**Es Pins £–££** Slap-bang in the middle of the beach, this lovely snack bar wouldn't look out of place on the Sunset Strip in San Antonio. Dark rattan chairs and sofas with comfy cushions look out to sea. Snacks, tapas and steaks are served at lunch and in the evening, while the bar is open all day. **ⓐ** In the middle of the beach **ⓛ** 10.00–24.00 daily

**Pura Vida £–££** This well-situated bar and restaurant serves everything from snacks to international food, and prides itself on its fresh fish dishes. **ⓐ** Platja Niu Blau, on the way to Santa Eulària from Es Canar **ⓣ** 971 33 97 72 **ⓦ** www.puravida-ibiza.com **ⓛ** 11.00–24.00 daily

**Las Arenas ££** Las Arenas has a varied menu ranging from steaks and chicken to fresh fish and paella. **ⓐ** Hostal Las Arenas, next to the bakery/pâtisserie, near the ferry terminus **ⓣ** 971 33 07 90 **ⓦ** www.lasarenasibiza.com **ⓛ** 08.30–24.00 daily

**New Wave ££** Hidden away in a quiet street in Es Canar, this place has three bars, indoor and outdoor dining, a video room, music and a menu of simple but substantial barbecue food such as steak, chicken, jacket potatoes and salads. ⓐ Can Soldat, Es Canar ⓣ 971 33 27 78 ⓛ 21.00–06.00 daily

**Pizzeria La Strada ££** There is a great choice of home-made pizza and other Italian dishes, plus grilled local fish. There's a children's menu too. Regulars are offered a liqueur by the owner, while children are offered a sweet at the end of the meal. ⓐ Edificio Manila, Avinguda Punta Arabi, on the right, heading towards Punta Arabi ⓣ 971 33 04 74 ⓛ 12.00–15.30 & 19.00–24.00 daily

## AFTER DARK

### Restaurants & bars
**Bar Tipic** Beach bar with a family atmosphere where you can enjoy an evening drink. ⓐ Platja es Cana ⓣ 971 33 04 26 ⓛ 09.00–until late daily

**The Red Lion** The first English pub in Es Canar – with karaoke, bingo and 'Play Your Cards Right'. ⓐ Avinguda Punta Arabi ⓣ 971 31 90 09 ⓛ 22.00–until late daily (May–Oct)

### Clubs
**Kancela** is another little bar/club in the town. ⓐ Avinguda d'Es Canar ⓛ 20.00–04.00 daily

**Popeye's** pub-club has nightly live entertainment, darts, pool and a British menu. Just below Popeye's is a club. ⓐ On the road from Es Canar to the Miami Hotel and Calanova Platja, Es Canar ⓣ 971 33 90 67 ⓛ 09.00–04.00 daily

# Cala Llonga

The small resort of Cala Llonga is popular with families and couples. The pine-backed cove has shallow, safe water, which is great for children. Ideally situated on the east coast between the interesting centres of Santa Eulària and Ibiza Town, Cala Llonga makes a good starting point for day excursions. It is a relaxed place and there is a small range of shops and restaurants to choose from. Small ferries run between the beach at Cala Llonga and Ibiza Town or Santa Eulària, which you can also reach by bus.

## BEACHES

The main beach is sheltered with fine sand and shallow water that only reaches a depth of 1 m (3 ft) when 25 m (27 yds) from the shore. Tucked away about 700 m (765 yds) to the south is the small pebble beach of **Sol d'en Serra**. It's a peaceful spot with a snack bar, away from the crowds of the main beach.

## THINGS TO SEE & DO

### Horse riding
Beginners and experienced riders can take a short trip or a half-day ride into the surrounding countryside.
🄐 Easy Rider, Sol d'en Serra, 400 m (438 yds) from Cala Llonga beach
🕐 971 19 65 11 🕐 10.00–13.00 & 17.00–sunset, daily

### Mini-train
The Es Trenet mini-train meanders through the roads every day from outside the tourist information point to Santa Eulària. The scenic journey takes about two hours.
🄐 Departs from the tourist information point 🕐 Trains at 10.00, 12.00 & 17.00 daily

## Walking

You can walk over the mountains to Santa Eulària, about two hours away. It's incredibly scenic with great views. As a designated 'Falcon Route' (see page 103) it is clearly signposted. Either take a taxi back or return along the more inland path for a change of scenery. Make sure you take plenty of water with you, cover your head, and don't set off in the heat of the day.

⬤ *The cove at Cala Llonga*

## SHOPPING

There are several small supermarkets, newsagents and off-licences on the road behind the beach. Every Thursday evening the Hippy Market fills the pedestrian area behind the beach and sells everything from jewellery to clothes and souvenirs (18.00–23.00). Santa Eulària, the nearest town with plenty of shops and restaurants, is only ten minutes away by taxi. Similarly, Ibiza Town is a 20-minute ride away.

### Watersports

Pedaloes are available for hire on the beach. Rumbo Azul Dive Centre offers PADI courses and daily outings for certified divers.
ⓐ Hotel Sirenis Playa Imperial ⓣ 971 19 66 25 ⓦ www.rumboazul.com

## TAKING A BREAK

### Restaurants

**Cafeteria Equus £** Serving basic snacks and meals such as sandwiches and omelettes, the café also has a couple of computers for internet use as well as being wi-fi enabled. ⓐ Carretera de Cala Llonga 133 08.00–22.00 daily

**La Cantina 'Sols' Bar £** Serves traditional Sunday lunch, steak and onion and English pies. There is a cocktail list and family games. ⓐ Just behind the main beach ⓣ 971 19 65 88 12.00–15.00 & 19.00–24.00 Thur–Tues, 19.00–24.00 Wed

**Restaurant Cala Llonga £** Choose from fresh fish, shellfish, good meat dishes or just a snack at this restaurant, which has sports TV. ⓐ On the left of the beach as you look out to sea ⓣ 971 19 64 74 09.30–16.00 & 19.00–23.30 daily

**Restaurante Valentino £** Pizzas and pasta are served in this lovely little Italian restaurant, perfect for a meal for two. ⓐ Edificio Sol Y Mar (in the lane behind the Up 'n' Inn) ❶ 971 19 64 79 🕓 18.30–01.00 daily

**Sol d'en Serra Restaurant ££** This secluded restaurant has a terrace and sun-loungers. A full international menu with Mediterranean and Asian influences is offered. ⓐ Overlooking the small beach at Platja de Sol d'en Serra, at the top of the slope ❶ 971 19 61 76 🕓 12.00–17.00 & 20.00–01.00 daily

## AFTER DARK

Cala Llonga is a quiet resort but it does have a couple of bars that stay open late.

**Mister Cairo's Show Bar** puts on live cabaret nightly with quizzes, bingo and karaoke in between acts. Afterwards, the music is turned up and you can keep dancing until 04.00. ⓐ Carretera de Cala Llonga 🕓 19.00–04.00 daily. Happy Hour is 19.00–21.00

**Up 'n' Inn** has karaoke on Wednesday and live entertainment most nights of the week. ⓐ Carretera de Cala Llonga ❶ 971 19 65 69 ⓦ www.up-inn.com 🕓 11.00–24.00 daily

🔺 *Cala Llonga is a relaxed resort*

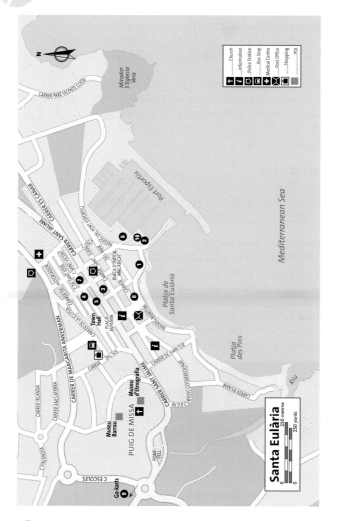

Santa Eulària

| Church |
| Information |
| Police Station |
| Bus Stop |
| Medical Centre |
| Post Office |
| Shopping |
| POI |

Mediterranean Sea

Port Esportiu

Platja de
Santa Eulària

Platja
des Pins

Riu

Minador
S'Església
Vella

CARRER PARE VICENTE COSTA

CARRER ES CANÀR

CARRER SANT JAUME

PASSEIG DEL PORT ESPORTIU

MAR I SOL

PLAÇA D'ESPAÑA

SANT JOSE
CONILLERA
PINTOR VIZCAI
SANT LLORENÇ

PLAÇA D'ISIDOR MACABICH

MARE DE DÉU DEL MAR

PASSEIG S'ALAMERA

CALVARI

CARRER DE MARGARITA ANKERMAN

CARRER DE JUAN TUR

CARRER DE SOL

CARRER IRLANDA

CARRER ANGLATERRA

FINLÀNDIA

CISTOY GOTARREDO

CARRER SANT JAIME

AV D R C

CARRER RIUMAR

PONT
VELL

Town
Hall

Museu
Barrau

Museu
d'Etnografía

PUIG DE MISSA

Go-karts

C ESCOLES

Santa Eulària

0        250 metres
0        250 yards

62

# Santa Eulària (Santa Eulalía)

Santa Eulària – also known as Santa Eulalía – is many people's favourite place on Ibiza. It has managed to retain its identity and local culture while also embracing holidaymakers.

Santa Eulària is the third-largest town on Ibiza, after the capital and San Antonio, and so the streets beyond the promenade are also filled with shops, bars and cafés, pleasant squares, and some of the best restaurants on the island – especially in the port area.

The main street, Carrer Sant Jaume, is lined with trees and is a good place to wander. Behind this, Carrer Sant Vicent is known as the 'street of restaurants' because of its variety of eating places. Plaça Espanya is a pleasant spot to sit and watch the world go by as it's filled with flowers, fountains, street-sellers and painters.

## THINGS TO SEE & DO

### Boat trips
Small ferries run throughout the day between the harbour at Santa Eulària to Ibiza Town, Cala Llonga, Es Canar and the Hippy Market as well as the island of Formentera.
ⓐ **Servitur** between the port and the promenade ❶ 971 33 22 51 (information only) ☀ May–Oct

### Diving
Learn to dive and take your PADI certification to discover some of Ibiza's underwater scenery. Join in night dives and visit old wrecks.
ⓐ Port Esportiu ❶ 971 33 84 59/620 68 67 68
ⓦ www.aquadivingcenter.com

### Go-karts
The racetrack has plenty of karts for all ages from those for children aged 4–7 right up to adult karts.
ⓐ Carretera Ibiza-Santa Eulària Km 6 ❶ 971 31 77 44

⬤ *Whitewashed buildings in Santa Eulària*

---

Ⓦ www.gokartssantaeulalia.com Ⓛ 10.00–21.30 daily (Apr–Oct);
11.00–20.30 Sat & Sun (Nov–Mar)

### Miniature train

Take a ride into the countryside on the Santa Eulalia Express, which toots
through the town and takes in the Ethnological Museum. The journey
lasts almost two hours and includes a free drink at a refreshment stop
halfway around.
ⓐ Departs from Town Hall (Ajuntament) Ⓣ 605 89 13 87 Ⓛ 10.00, 12.00
& 16.00 daily

### Museu d'Etnografia (The Ethnological Museum)

This tiny museum traces the town's history and has traditional
costumes and jewellery on display as well as farming implements and
musical instruments.

Can Ros, Puig de Missa  971 33 28 45  10.00–14.00 & 17.30–20.00 Mon–Sat, 11.00–13.30 Sun (Apr–Sept); 10.00–14.00 Tues–Sat, 11.00–13.30 Sun (Oct–Mar)  Closed 20 Dec–20 Jan. Admission charge

### Pont Vell (The Roman Bridge)

As you drive in from Ibiza Town, you will see this recently renovated bridge, built by the Romans in AD 70.

### Puig de Missa

Follow the signs to this hill above the town. It's only about 90 m (295 ft) high but has great views because the land around is mostly flat. At the top is the 16th-century church dedicated to Santa Eulària, the Ethnological Museum (see opposite) and the Museu Laureà Barrau dedicated to the eponymous Catalan modernist painter ( Museu Laureà Barrau, Puig de Missa 10.00–14.00 Tues–Fri, closed Sat–Mon Admission charge).

## TAKING A BREAK

### Restaurants & cafés

There are three main restaurant areas: one along the promenade, one along Carrer Sant Vicent and one at the port.

**Gelateria Miretti £ ❶** Grab an ice cream or sit down and enjoy an ice-cream cocktail. Passeig Marítim 971 33 18 22 09.00–24.00 daily

**Mirage £ ❷** Traditional English breakfasts. The evenings pick up a notch with live entertainment nightly. Port Esportiu 971 33 25 40 09.00–03.00 daily

**Que Tal Café £ ❸** Mingle with the locals in this busy café on the main street. Croissants, doughnuts and pain au chocolat as well as baguettes, toasted sandwiches and fresh juices. Carrer Sant Juan 56 971 33 67 95 08.00–22.30 daily Free wi-fi

**Ca Na Ribes ££** ❹   Local dishes such as skate in almond sauce and international food. Courtyard garden inside and ice-cream parlour next door. ⓐ Carrer Sant Vicent 44 ❶ 971 33 00 06 ❶ 13.00–15.30 & 19.00–23.30 daily, closed Wed (Sept–July)

**Celler C'an Pere ££** ❺   Family owned and offering both local specialities and regular fare. Good seafood too. Choose lobster fresh from the tank. ⓐ Carrer Sant Jaume 63 ❶ 971 33 00 56 ❶ 13.00–15.30 & 19.00–24.00 daily, closed Thur lunch

**Sa Llesca ££** ❻   Lovely terrace and chill-out area by the stone tower in the port; specialities include fresh salads, pâté, cold meats and cheeses. ⓐ Port Esportiu ❶ 971 33 62 28 ❶ 19.00–03.00 Tues–Sun, closed Mon

**Pato Pekin ££** ❼   Spring rolls, fried rice, crispy duck, chop suey and all your favourite Chinese dishes are served to diners in this authentic Chinese restaurant. ⓐ Carrer Sant Vicent 37 ❶ 971 33 11 64 ❶ 11.30–16.00 & 18.30–24.00 daily ❶ Takeaway service

**Pier 1 ££** ❽   Fish and chips shop along the promenade. ⓐ Passeig Maritim ❶ 971 33 15 29 ❶ 10.00–23.00 daily

## AFTER DARK

### Restaurants & bars
**Bambuddha Grove** ❾   Chill out at this lounge bar in an authentic Thai building and enjoy an Asian–Mediterranean menu. ⓐ Carretera Sant Joan Km 8.5 ❶ 971 19 75 10 ⓦ www.bambuddha.com ❶ 20.00–01.00 daily

**Guarana** ❿   As well as dance music on weeknights, Guarana is renowned for live music and jazz and blues on Sundays. ⓐ Puerto Deportivo ⓦ www.guaranaibiza.com ❶ 20.00–until late daily

❶ *Ibiza is a paradise for sailing*

# EXCURSIONS
Out & about

# Ibiza's club scene

The island has one of the best club scenes in the world. The venues, massive-capacity places where much money has been spent on the interiors, are not equalled even in London. England's best DJs are brought to the island throughout the season. The result is high-quality music in beautiful venues with crowds that always seem to want more. While some clubs cater mainly for British tourists, the larger venues, such as Privilege, El Divino and Pacha, draw more of a European crowd.

## THE BALEARIC SOUND

The Balearic Sound, known the world over, came out of Ibiza and its sister islands in the Balearics after house music first took off in England. Club-goers picked up on the music, which combined house with the more rhythmic sound of flamenco and Spanish folk music. You'll hear it almost everywhere you go, and particularly at the sunset bars.

● *A street parade; one of the many ways clubs grab attention*

## PROMOTERS

It is the promoters and their DJs that make a night, not the venue. The most popular clubs normally have one big night of the week, such as the legendary **Manumission** (whose future is uncertain at the time of writing), which changes club and night from season to season. Check posters, flyers and any of the free magazines that can easily be found at many shops at the port of Ibiza.

## OPENING TIMES

Most clubs open their doors around midnight and get going at about 02.00. Due to a new law restricting opening hours, the early morning 'After Party' is now a thing of the past. Clubs can now only open between 16.30 and 06.00. Many of the big nights have pre-parties where people meet to have a few drinks and get in the mood. Keep your eyes open for promotions and discounts on tickets.

## OPENING AND CLOSING PARTIES

Opening parties are in the first week of June. The season winds down in about the third week of September when many of the club nights have their closing parties. The clubs themselves tend to stay open until the first week of October when they will go out with a big bang – until it all starts again next year.

## COST

Entrance to clubs is expensive and can cost around €50. Admission often includes a drink, and you will want to take advantage of this as even the price of a bottle of water is exorbitant in some places (€10 is not uncommon). Buy your ticket in advance from a recognised bar or stand and you will normally make a saving of about 15 per cent and a taxi is often thrown in.

Many promoters at the big clubs will refund the cost of a taxi as long as there are three or more people together. Look out for details on promotional literature and tickets.

## THE DISCO BUS

Calling at the main nightclubs and hotels, there are four bus services which run all night:

Red route: Every 30 mins from San Antonio to Privilege, Amnesia, Pacha and Ibiza Port.

Blue route: Every 30 mins from Platja d'en Bossa to Space, Ibiza Port and Pacha.

Green route: Every hour from Es Canar to Santa Eulària and Ibiza Port.

Yellow route: Every hour from San Antonio to Port d'es Torrent.

It is a cheap alternative to taxis (€3 one way or book of 5 tickets for €12), which can be difficult to find in summer. Ask at your local tourist office for details. See Ⓦ www.discobus.es for details.

## VENUES

**Amnesia** Renowned for its weekly foam parties. ⓐ Sant Rafel, on the road between Ibiza Town and San Antonio ⓣ 971 79 80 41 Ⓦ www.amnesia.es

**El Divino** This stylish club has an outdoor seated area with views of Ibiza Town and harbour. It puts on a boat to take punters from the bars in Ibiza. ⓐ Puerto Deportivo, Ibiza Town ⓣ 971 31 83 38 Ⓦ www.eldivino-ibiza.com

**Eden** The youngest megaclub on the block (it opened in 1999), Eden now has some of the best club nights in Ibiza. And it's right in the centre of San Antonio (see page 39). ⓐ Carrer Salvador Espriu (off Avinguda Doctor Fleming), San Antonio ⓣ 971 80 32 40 Ⓦ www.edenibiza.com

**Pacha** Top DJs from all over the world get Pacha pumping every night for a style-savvy crowd. ⓐ Avinguda 8 d'Agost, Ibiza Town ⓣ 971 31 36 12 Ⓦ www.pacha.com

**Es Paradis** This club is unique. A huge venue, it has different floors with marble columns and giant plants that reach up to the glass pyramid

roof, which can be opened to the elements. It is most famous for its Fiesta del Agua on Wednesday and Saturday, when the dance floor becomes a swimming pool at dawn. There are also several bars, pool tables and a central dancing podium (see page 39 for details).

**Privilege** The world's largest nightclub with a capacity of 10,000.
ⓐ Sant Rafel, on the road between Ibiza Town and San Antonio
ⓣ 971 19 80 86 ⓦ www.privilegeibiza.com

**Space** Once renowned for its 'After Parties', this is still one of the best clubs on the island (see page 27).
ⓐ Platja d'en Bossa ⓣ 971 39 67 93 ⓦ www.space-ibiza.es
ⓛ 22.00–06.00 (Mon–Sat), 16.30–06.00 (Sun)

**Summum**

At the Summum Club (see page 43) in San Antonio Bay you can listen to an alternative to house – anything from jazz to flamenco. Summum is an upmarket venue and one of the very first clubs to be established on the island.

🔺 *Inside Amnesia*

◔ *Enjoy a drink on the Sunset Strip*

# Evening entertainment

Many tour companies offer a package of events that changes weekly or fortnightly. Some nights are arranged to give you a range of pre-club entertainment, with discounted entry and free drinks in bars and clubs. Other events are designed to keep the whole family entertained and are suitable for children. Here are some of the typical tours on offer.

## Foam parties

Foam and water parties are a bit of an Ibiza institution, although not as popular as they once were. The foam or water is released from the ceiling to soak the people on the dance floor, whose reaction can be anything from skidding to stripping. The dance floor at **Es Paradis** actually fills with water and becomes a swimming pool.

Es Paradis in San Antonio has a 'Water Festival' twice a week in summer. **Amnesia** at Sant Rafel holds a twice-weekly foam party, while **Privilege**, also in Sant Rafel, holds a weekly foam session.

## Funfair

Funfair with amusements, dodgems, bungee rides and much more entertainment for all the family.

ⓐ Avinguda Dr Fleming, close to Es Paradis

## Kiwi Fiesta – Hangi Night

A different way to spend the night with the whole family together. Every Thursday in an old finca; try a Maori dish.

ⓐ Can Truy, Santa Eulària ① 971 32 50 73 ① 20.00 Thur

❶ Special Kiddies Club

## Murphy's Irish Bar

Enjoy a night out, Irish style. You will be served dinner and drinks in an authentic Irish pub where there is draught Guinness®, Irish whiskey and lots of fun. Suitable for all the family, this event includes a cabaret,

● *The harbour promenade in Sant Antoni*

competitions and a live band. Pubs in Platja d'en Bossa, San Antonio and Es Canar.
Ⓦ www.murphyspub-ibiza.com Ⓛ 21.00–06.00 daily

## OTHER NIGHTLIFE AREAS

Ibiza Town and San Antonio are, without doubt, the two places that contain the biggest concentration of nightlife, ranging from the avant-garde, where you can hear and dance to the latest music, to the pleasant terraces and bars of the leisure marinas and fishing ports. It must be said, however, that the nightlife is not just confined to the setting of the Ibizan capital's port. Every holiday resort has its own entertainment for all tastes.

**Blue Marlin £££** The hip young crowd hangs out at this beach bar during the day where the resident DJ belts out house tracks. The party really gets going after dark. ⓐ Cala Jondal Ⓣ 971 41 01 17
Ⓦ www.bluemarlinibiza.com Ⓛ 10.00–06.00 daily

### Lounge bars

A number of smart lounge bars can be found at various locations throughout the island, often in more rural areas. The easiest way to reach many of these is by taxi or rental car.

### Sant Antoni

The main Sunset Strip is the place to start your evening with a leisurely cocktail and a soundtrack of ambient, chill-out or soulful house to unwind to (see page 37). On the harbour promenade, fountains dance as music is played, every night at about 21.00.

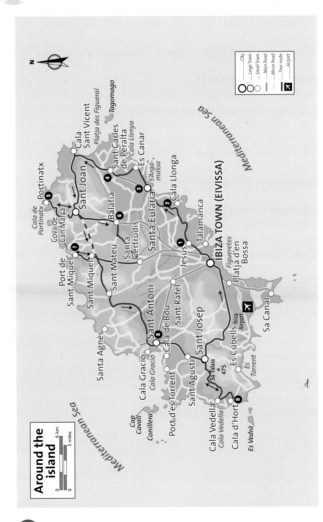

Around the island

0 | 6 km
0 | 3 miles
Mediterranean Sea

Mediterranean Sea

Cap Cavall
Conillera

Santa Agnès

Port de Sant Miquel
Sant Miquel
Cova de Can Marçà
Port de Portinatx
Cala de Portinatx
Portinatx
Cala Sant Vicent
Sant Vicent
Tagomago
Platja des Figueral

Cala Sant Joan
Sant Joan
Sant Carles de Peralta
Es Canar
Cala Llenya
S'Arga-massa

Balàfia
Santa Gertrudis
Santa Eulària
Cala Llonga

Sant Mateu

Cala Gració
Cala Gració

Sant Antoni
Cala de Bou
Sant Rafel
Jesús
Talamanca
IBIZA TOWN (EIVISSA)

Mediterranean Sea

Port d'es Torrent
Sant Josep
Sant Agustí
Es Cubells
Es Torrent
Sa Talaia ▲ 475
Figueretes
Platja d'en Bossa
Ibiza Airport ✈
Sa Canal

Cala Vedella
Cala Vedella
Cala d'Hort
Es Vedrà

City
Large Town
Small Town
Main Road
Minor Road
Tour route
Airport

N

❶ ❷ ❸ ❹ ❺ ❻ ❼ ❽ ❾

# Around the island

Ibiza is very small and hiring a car for a few days will enable you to see most of it. There are small coves for beach-lovers to discover, and some of the inland villages are beautiful. The following suggested route takes in many of the best places – and, while exploring, you might find a resort for your next holiday on Ibiza.

Don't book a car too early in your holiday. Wait until you've seen what days the various optional excursions are on. You can usually negotiate a better rate if you want the vehicle for more than one day.

## THE ROUTE

This circular route starts and ends in Ibiza Town, although of course you can join it anywhere you like. Depending on how long you stop at each point, this route could take a whole day.

### ❶ Jesús

On leaving Ibiza Town (see page 15) take the road marked Santa Eulària. As you leave the town behind, watch for the right turning to Jesús – a name that's hard to miss. In fact you might like to stop in this tiny hamlet and visit its church, Nostra Mare de Jesús (🕒 09.30–12.30, 16.30–19.00 daily). Inside is a painting of the Virgin and Child, thought to date from the 16th century and widely regarded as the greatest work of art on the island – it is an unusual depiction of Mary breastfeeding the baby Jesus.

### ❷ Cala Llonga

On leaving Jesús head for the small resort of Cala Llonga (see page 58), with its lovely beach. Take a break at the secluded, pine-scented cove or continue on to rejoin the main road heading for Santa Eulària. As you approach the town, look on your left for the hill of Puig de Missa topped by a white church. On your right, as you cross the only river in the Balearic Islands (it's usually dried up), look out for the Pont Vell (Old Roman Bridge).

### ❸ Santa Eulària

Santa Eulària (see page 63) is well worth a long stop, then afterwards carry on to Es Canar (see page 53), a smaller resort that's still quite lively. Use the ring road on Wednesday mornings, unless you can be very early, as the weekly Hippy Market attracts traffic from all over Ibiza.

### ❹ Sant Carles de Peralta

Leave Es Canar the way you came in, and take the right-hand turn where the main road turns sharp left. This leads through some lovely scenery to the attractive little village of Sant Carles de Peralta, a popular hippy haunt in the 1960s. There is an interesting Hippy Market here at Las Dalias on Saturdays and on Monday nights. Beyond here, the road winds through pine-covered hills and down to the tiny resort of Cala Sant Vicent (see page 48), with a nice beach.

### ❺ Portinatx

Head back uphill and take the road to Sant Joan, another pleasant town. Beyond here take a right turn to the much busier holiday resort of Portinatx (see page 44), a good spot for lunch – the Cas Mallorqui restaurant is well recommended (see page 47).

### ❻ Balafia

Take the road back towards Ibiza Town and, just beyond the turning to Sant Joan, you have a decision to make. If you're a nervous driver, take the first right turn to Sant Miquel. If you are a bit braver and fancy a bit of adventure, carry on and watch carefully for the right turn to Balafia, almost opposite the turning to Es Canar. Bump along the rough track to Balafia. Its Moorish heritage, ancient buildings and fortified towers make it one of the most unusual inland villages. Carry on through it and pick up the better road to Santa Gertrudis. This pretty village is an ideal place to stop and have a drink and eat some olives at one of the pavement cafés.

🔺 *Ibiza has many coves for beach-lovers*

The bay of Cala d'Hort

**❼ Port de Sant Miquel**

Take the road towards Sant Miguel to its port and visit the caves.

**❽ Sant Antoni (San Antonio)**

Return to the town of Sant Miquel and turn right to San Antonio (see page 33).

**❾ Cala d'Hort**

Leave San Antonio and head towards the little village of Sant Agustí on the Sant Josep road, but before you reach Sant Josep itself look for the right turn to Cala d'Hort (see page 28). This little bay is well worth the detour, with its view of the offshore island of Es Vedrà. When you leave you can either retrace your route or take a right turn marked Sant Josep, an interesting little village worth a visit. Both routes are similar in distance, and take you back to the main road where you turn right to head back into Ibiza Town.

## TAKING A BREAK

### Restaurants & bars

**Santa Gertrudis £** This has several bars that serve delicious sandwiches and tapas. ⓐ Plaça de l'Església Santa Gertrudis ❶ 971 19 70 57

**Bon Lloc ££** This bar and restaurant is a pleasant place to stop for a drink, snack or meal. ⓐ Jesús, on the main road running through the village ❶ 971 31 18 13 ❷ Bar 07.00–01.00 daily; Restaurant 12.00–16.00, 19.00–24.00 daily

**Cas Pages ££** Traditional Mallorcan cooking such as rice with pork plus grills. ⓐ Carretera Sant Carles, Pont de s'Argentera ❶ 971 31 90 29 ❶ No reservations & no credit cards

**Ama Lur £££** For those wishing to splash out a bit more, this upmarket restaurant offers excellent service, a good selection of fine wines and an

◓ *Ibiza Town, overlooking the marina*

award-winning Basque menu. ⓐ Carretera Ibiza-Sant Miquel Km 2.3,
2.3 km (1½ miles) on the road from Ibiza Town to Santa Gertrudis
ⓣ 971 31 45 54 ⓦ www.restauranteamalur.com ⓛ 20.00–24.00 daily
ⓘ Closed Wed (winter)

## ISLAND TOURS

Take in the island's varied highlights in a tailor-made tour that
has something for everyone. You could watch potters and shop at a
ceramic factory, visit a distillery to try as you buy, and explore beautiful
Dalt Vila (see page 17) and the shops at the heart of Ibiza Town. There
are also opportunities to take photos at the dramatic island of Es Vedrà
and the unusual landscape of the salt flats. This is a relaxed way to
get to know the island and a whole day is required. If you want to see
everything in more depth, however, divide the island in two – one half
one day, the other half the next. Visit the local tourist office or ask your
holiday representative to find out about tour operators.

## CRUISES

Sail along the coast of Ibiza and enjoy secluded coves from the comfort
of a boat. The glass-bottomed boats allow you to see brightly coloured
fish and other underwater creatures. These cruises tend to last a full day,
with drinks served on board and lunch at a beach where you can also
swim. Some companies offer themed cruises such as a pirate trip,
complete with a treasure hunt on the beach.

**Cruceros Portmany** ⓐ From San Antonio to Es Vedrà. Departs from the
waterfront promenade near the Egg ⓣ 971 34 34 71
ⓦ www.crucerosportmany.com

**Ulises Cat** ⓐ Platja d'en Bossa ⓦ www.ulisesibiza.com ⓛ 09.50 & 11.10
from Figueretes, 10.00 & 11.00 from Platja d'en Bossa, returning at 17.00
& 19.00

◆ *Formentera has many stretches of white, sandy beach*

# Formentera

Ibiza's nearest neighbour in the Balearic Islands is a short, but sometimes choppy, hop away. It takes just over an hour on the conventional ferries, and half an hour on the faster catamaran service.

Formentera is a world away from Ibiza. There is tourism here but on a much smaller scale, and the island has a more peaceful atmosphere, with its wonderful stretches of white, sandy beach. The island is very rural, with a scattering of small villages and a population of only 9,000 people – compared to 47,000 in Ibiza Town alone. The island is flatter and less wooded than Ibiza, but there is one dramatic height – La Mola at 192 m (630 ft). At Cap de Barbaría, on Formentera's southern tip, you can stand on the cliff edge, with its lighthouse, watchtowers and Bronze Age remains, and look south to the coast of North Africa.

Ferries run 07.30–20.30 almost every hour. In high season the frequency increases. The boats go from the western end of the harbour in Ibiza Town, and you buy your tickets in advance inside the building there (ⓐ Estación Marítima ⓣ 966 42 87 00 ⓛ 09.00–21.00). Balearia car ferries leave from the Ibiza Old Town end of the port and need booking in advance (ⓣ 902 16 01 80 ⓦ www.balearia.com).

If you're making your own way to Formentera, rather than joining an organised excursion, then you don't need to book a return ticket. The savings are very small and you are restricted to that particular ferry line's services when another boat may be more convenient for bringing you back. Pick up a collection of timetables for all the ferry companies at the Estación Marítima in Ibiza.

## BEACHES

There are several excellent beaches on Formentera, and these tend to be quieter than the ones on Ibiza. The island's only real resort is at Es Pujols. **Platja de Migjorn** is a popular pebbly beach, while **Platja de ses Illetes** is probably the most attractive beach, with dunes and a long stretch of sand, not far from La Savina.

## THINGS TO SEE & DO

### Ca Na Costa

If you're on the road from the port to Es Pujols (see opposite), take a look at what is said to be one of the most important archaeological finds in the Balearic Islands. It is a stone circle marking a megalithic burial tomb, dated to about 2000 BC. Some of the human remains, pottery and other items that were found here can be seen in the Museu Arqueològic de Dalt Vila (see page 17).

### Cap de Barbaría

A visit to the southern tip of the island gives a glimpse of the rugged life faced by the islanders in the past. You pass through a goat-filled landscape before finally reaching an isolated lighthouse.

### Green routes

A network of ancient tracks can be followed on foot or by bicycle. This forms one of the island's major attractions. Hire a bike when you arrive at La Savina.

### La Mola

The cliffs and lighthouse at the eastern tip of the island offer terrific views, not just out to sea but back over Formentera and its pinewood.

### TRANSPORT

There is no airport on the island, and no plans to build one. This is part of the reason why it is so peaceful here and tourism is not on the same scale as neighbouring Ibiza. The island is tiny – only about 19 km (12 miles) long – so the best way to explore it is by bike, as you can cover most places in a day. There are specially designated cycle routes and not too many cars. Mopeds and cars can also be hired at the harbour of La Savina. The local bus system is erratic and cannot be relied on, but there are plenty of taxis.

The cliffs at La Mola plunge dramatically into the sea. As there is no barrier or warning sign and nothing to break a fall, be very careful, especially with young children.

## Es Pujols

The island's main resort is tiny by Ibizan standards, but it has a decent beach and a good choice of eating places for lunch.

## Las Salinas

Formentera's salt pans are not used now, as the salt trade has all but died out. However, they provide a good refuge for wildlife and occasionally even flamingoes have been reported here.

◆ *Cap de Barbaria on Formentera*

◐ *The Formentera coastline*

## SHOPPING

Apart from the shops selling local products in Sant Francesc, you will mostly find the inevitable souvenir shops elsewhere on the island. Look out for island knitwear from the **Mercería La Mola** shop at El Pilar.

There is a daily **Hippy Market** at Es Pujols from 18.00 until late, and in the capital, Sant Francesc, from 09.00 to 14.00, as well as a **crafts market** on Wednesday and Sunday (May–Oct) from 16.00 until sunset at El Pilar de la Mola.

## Sant Francesc

The island's capital is only small, but it's the best place for local souvenirs such as knitwear, ceramics, cheese, honey and Formentera's own *hierbas* drinks. There is a small ethnological museum showing the island's history. ⓐ Museu d'Etnografia de Formentera, Carrer Jaume I, Sant Francesc de Formentera ⓣ 971 32 26 70 ⓛ 10.00–14.00 & 17.00–19.00 Mon–Fri (summer); 10.00–14.00 Mon–Sat (winter)

## Watersports

There are sailing, windsurfing and waterskiing opportunities and excellent waters for diving on the island. Ask for details at the tourist office at the port when you arrive from the ferry, or consult the free magazine, *touribsport*. Some of the beaches have pedaloes. ⓦ www.touribisport.com

## TAKING A BREAK

### Restaurants

For such a small island, Formentera has a wide variety of eating places specialising mainly in locally caught fish.

**La Barca ££** Stylish and near the beach, with an outdoor terrace. Fish and other dishes are served. ⓐ Es Pujols ⓣ 971 32 85 02 ⓛ 13.00–15.30 & 20.30–24.00 daily

**Bellavista ££** A good choice, right in the port of La Savina, with island food and a wider menu to cater for the tourist trade. ⓐ Port of La Savina ⓣ 971 32 22 36 ⓛ 12.00–24.00 daily

**El Mirador ££** Elevated restaurant with amazing views over land and sea. Fish a speciality. ⓐ La Mola Km 14.3 ⓣ 971 32 70 37 ⓛ 13.00–16.00 & 19.00–23.00 daily

**Pequeña Isla ££** In Es Pilar and not to be missed if you want fresh fish. Try a typical island dish such as *calamar a la Bruna* – squid fried with local sausage, potatoes and peppers. Wider menu also available. ⓐ El Pilar de la Mola ⓣ 971 32 70 68 ⓛ 13.30–15.30 & 20.30–00.30 daily ⓦ www.pequenaisla.com

**Can Rafalet £££** Great views from the terrace restaurant in a quiet setting. A good variety of seafood, fish and rice dishes. ⓐ Es Caló de Sant Agustí ⓣ 971 32 70 77 ⓛ 13.00–15.30 & 20.00–23.00 daily

**Juan y Andrea £££** Right on the sands of Platja de ses Illetes, lobster and rice specialities are served to a jet-set clientele such as Bill Gates and Bill Clinton. ⓐ On the beach at Platja des ses Illetes ⓣ 971 18 71 30 ⓦ www.juanyandrea.com ⓛ 13.00–02.00 daily (May–Sept)

## AFTER DARK

### Restaurant & club
**Blue Bar** The resident DJ at this restaurant and beach club plays chillout and house music into the night. ⓐ Carretera a la Mola Km 7.9, Platja Migjorn ⓣ 971 18 70 11 ⓦ www.bluebarformentera.com ⓛ 12.00–24.00 daily (May–Oct)

---

◖ *Relax at a sunset bar at the end of the day*

 LIFESTYLE
The Ibizan way

◆ *Ibiza offers a great choice of restaurants*

# Food & drink

With around 2,000 bars and restaurants, finding somewhere to eat and drink in Ibiza is not a problem. As well as local and Spanish food, there are also many French, Italian and Chinese restaurants. Other establishments serve 'international' menus, including typically British dishes.

## MEAL TIMES

Because Ibiza is a fishing and farming island, where people have traditionally needed to get up early, meal times are not quite as late as they are on the Spanish mainland. Lunch is usually served from about 13.30 to 15.00, with dinner from 20.00 to 23.00, but you'll always find places open if you want to eat earlier or later.

## IBIZAN DISHES

Look out for typical dishes. *Sofrit pages* is made with lamb, potatoes, saffron and local sausages. *Sobrassada* (paprika-flavoured cured pork sausage) and *utiffara* (aniseed-flavoured pork sausage) are also good in a *bocadillo* (sandwich). *Guisat de peix* is a delicious fish stew usually served as two courses – first the fish with boiled potatoes and *alioli* (garlic mayonnaise), and then a fish soup. Naturally, fresh fish is common, but it is more expensive than other dishes. However, this is your chance to try salmon, swordfish, fresh lobsters and shellfish at prices you would never get back home. A local favourite is squid, which often comes deep-fried in batter: *calamar a la romana*.

You can't come to Spain and not try a Spanish omelette (tortilla) at least once. In some places an omelette is a light snack for when you're not very hungry, but the Spanish version is a meal in itself, jam-packed with potatoes and with or without onions.

### Paella

You will see paella on almost every menu, so do give it a try at least once. Most places will only serve it for a minimum of two people, and to do it properly does take a little time, so be prepared to wait. Saffron rice is

cooked in a big iron pan, and it's actually the pan that's the paella, not the food. It will have vegetables and fish thrown in, and every place has its own version. Some of the seafood paellas are quite spectacular to look at, with prawns, shrimps, mussels and chunks of fish. Vegetarians take care: it's quite common to find meat in paella too.

### Desserts

A popular dessert is *greixonera*, a kind of bread pudding flavoured with lemon and cinnamon, and there are Ibizan versions of cheesecake (*flaó*) and crème caramel (*flan*), too, as well as plenty of fresh fruit.

### TAPAS

There are plenty of tapas bars around in the bigger towns, though not always in the smaller ones. The word *tapa* means a lid, and it comes from the custom of serving a titbit of food with a drink; the food would be placed in a saucer on top of the glass, like a lid. Tapas today are still nibbles, but you can make a whole meal of them if you like: seafood, chunks of meat, bits of fish, olives, salads and vegetables. If you're not sure what to ask for, go inside and just point at what you want.

### DRINKS

*Cervezas* (Spanish beers) are widely available, and are usually slightly stronger than British beers. Wine-lovers will have no shortage of choice, with good-quality Spanish wine such as Rioja, or the strong island wine called *vi pages*. Sangría is popular on Ibiza, but this mix of red wine, brandy, fruit juices and ice can vary from watery to having a kick like a mule. Spanish brandy isn't generally as smooth as the French version but is a lot cheaper, while Ibiza has many liqueurs worth trying, such as *frigola* and *hierbas*, both sweet and made from herbs. If you just want a fresh fruit juice, try *granizados*, served with crushed ice.

⬥ *Fishermen from Ibiza Town*

## Menu decoder

**Aceitunas aliñadas** Marinated olives

**Albóndigas de pescado** Fish cakes

**Albóndigas en salsa** Meatballs in (usually tomato) sauce

**Alioli** Garlic-flavoured mayonnaise served as an accompaniment to just about anything – a rice dish, vegetables, shellfish – or as a dip for bread

**Bistek or biftek** Beef steak *poco hecho*; is rare, *regular* is medium and *bien hecho* is well done

**Bocadillo** The Spanish sandwich, usually made of French-style bread

**Caldereta** Stew based on fish or lamb

**Caldo** Soup or broth

**Carne** Meat; *carne de ternera* is beef, *carne picada* is minced meat, *carne de cerdo* is pork, *carne de cordero* is lamb

**Chorizo** Cured, dry, red-coloured sausage made from chopped pork, paprika, spices, herbs and garlic

**Churros** Flour fritters cooked in spiral shapes in very hot fat and cut into strips, best dunked into hot chocolate

**Cordero asado** Roast lamb flavoured with lemon and white wine

**Embutidos charcutería** Pork meat preparations including *jamón* (ham), *chorizo* (see above), *salchichones* (sausages) and *morcillas* (black pudding)

**Ensalada** Salad; the normal restaurant salad is composed of lettuce, onion, tomato and olives

**Ensalada mixta** As above, but with extra ingredients, such as boiled egg, tuna fish or asparagus

**Escabeche** Sauce of fish, meat or vegetables cooked in wine and vinegar and left to go cold

**Estofado de buey** Beef stew, made with carrots and turnips, or with potatoes

**Fiambre** Any type of cold meat such as ham, *chorizo*, etc.

**Flan** Caramel custard, the national dessert of Spain

**Fritura** A fry-up, as in *fritura de pescado* – different kinds of fried fish

**Gambas** Prawns; *gambas a la plancha* are grilled, *gambas al ajillo* are fried with garlic and *gambas con gabardina* deep-fried in batter

**Gazpacho andaluz** Cold soup (originally from Andalucía) made from tomatoes,

cucumbers, peppers, bread, garlic and olive oil

**Gazpacho manchego** Hot dish made with meat (chicken or rabbit) and unleavened bread (not to be confused with *gazpacho andaluz*)

**Habas con jamón** Broad beans fried with diced ham (sometimes with chopped hard-boiled egg and parsley)

**Helado** Ice cream

**Jamón** Ham; *jamón serrano* and *jamón ibérico* (far more expensive) are dry cured, *jamón de york* is cooked ham

**Langostinos a la plancha** Large prawns grilled and served with vinaigrette or *alioli*; *langostinos a la marinera* are cooked in white wine

**Lenguado** Sole, often served cooked with wine and mushrooms

**Mariscos** Seafood, including shellfish

**Menestra** Dish of mixed vegetables cooked separately and combined before serving

**Menú del día** Set menu for the day at a fixed price; it may or may not include bread, wine and a dessert, but it doesn't usually include coffee

**Paella** Famous rice dish originally from Valencia but now made all over Spain; *paella valenciana* has chicken and rabbit, *paella de mariscos* is made with seafood, *paella mixta* combines meat and seafood

**Pan** Bread; *pan de molde* is sliced white bread, *pan integral* is wholemeal

**Pincho moruno** Pork kebab – spicy chunks of pork on a skewer

**Pisto** Spanish version of ratatouille, made with tomatoes, peppers, onions, garlic, courgettes and aubergines

**Pollo al ajillo** Chicken fried with garlic; *pollo a la cerveza* is cooked in beer, *pollo al chilindrón* is cooked with peppers, tomatoes and onions

**Salpicón de mariscos** Seafood salad

**Sopa de ajo** Delicious warming winter garlic soup thickened with bread, usually with a poached egg floating in it

**Tarta helada** Popular ice-cream cake served as dessert

**Tortilla española** Classic omelette, made with potatoes and eaten hot or cold; if you want a plain omelette ask for a *tortilla francesa*

**Zarzuela de pescado y mariscos** Stew made with white fish and shellfish in a tomato, wine and saffron stock

# Shopping

The two most important features of recent Ibizan life, the hippy invasion and the club scene, have both had their impact on the souvenir trade too. If you want something that says 'Ibiza', check out the fashions and the jewellery. Most visitors will visit one of the Hippy Markets, where there is so much handmade jewellery that even the fussiest buyer should find something to appeal.

● *A girl having her hair braided at San Carlos market*

## DRINK & TOBACCO

Although duty-free goods are no longer available in Spain, shop prices are lower here and you can take home as much as you like (provided it's for your own personal consumption) as Spain is a fellow member of the European Union. However, it now has to go in the hold and not as hand luggage so it will need to be safely packed. Peach schnapps, *hierbas* (the local herb spirit), cigarettes and many of your favourite spirits from home are cheaper here.

## FASHION

Even the racks of humdrum souvenir T-shirts will include some very stylish items indeed. Ibiza Town is the place to hunt out fashion designs. A T-shirt from one of the renowned clubs will go down very well with youngsters at home, and the major clubs have their own shops in the port in Ibiza. Spanish chains like Mango and Zara are much cheaper for women's fashion than in other countries.

## LEATHER GOODS

Sandals, shoes, bags, wallets and other leather and suede goods are generally well made and reasonably priced. Lots of the souvenir shops sell them, and many places have their own specialist shop with a resident leather-worker.

## POTTERY

You'll be amazed at the variety of pottery that's for sale on Ibiza, and even more amazed when you realise that no clay is available on the island. Clay is imported from mainland Spain and fired on Ibiza, but a lot of stuff is also imported and then sold as if it had been made here. Buy something because you like it and not because you have to have something made locally. Having said that, there are many local potters producing good work in their own workshops, while if you drive around you're sure to see lots of ceramic 'superstores' by the side of the road (they look a little like garden centres). These sell everything from thimbles to huge plant pots.

# Children

Although Ibiza attracts plenty of publicity for its club scene, it is still the perfect place for a family holiday if you choose the right resort. Many hotels provide organised children's clubs and activities. Even if they don't, there is likely to be a games room or swimming pool for the youngsters. Most resorts also have a children's funfair open during the school holidays. Portinatx and San Antonio have mini-golf for all ages.

## BOATS

Plenty of places also have glass-bottomed boats (San Antonio (see page 36) even has a glass-bottomed catamaran!) to take you out to look at the wildlife under the sea, and the Es Canar (see page 54) trip includes a look at a sunken ship for good measure.

## CAVES

The Aquarium Cap Blanc (see page 34) at Cala Gració just outside of San Antonio is great for kids with the illuminated grotto and aquarium inside the caves. Just outside of Cala Sant Miquel is the Can Marça Caves (see page 45), where you can tour the underground caverns and see prehistoric cave paintings.

## GO-KARTING

A go-kart track at Santa Eulària offers thrills by day and night and even has baby karts for kids (see page 63). There is another one near San Antonio (Karting San Antonio, see page 34).

ⓐ Go-Karts Santa Eulalia, Carretera Ibiza-Santa Eulària Km 6, on the road to Ibiza, 6 km (3¾ miles) from Santa Eulària ⓣ 971 31 77 44 ⓦ www.gokartssantaeulalia.com ⓛ 10.00–21.00 daily (Apr–Oct); 11.00–20.30 Sat & Sun (Nov–Mar)

## TRAINS

Several resorts have miniature and scenic trains that chug along the coast and into the countryside for a couple of hours, usually

with a free drink for everyone halfway around (see pages 35, 50, 58, 64).

## WATER PARK

Aguamar Water Park (see page 24) is well worth a day out.
ⓐ Platja d'en Bossa ❶ 971 39 67 90 ❷ 10.00–18.00 daily (Jun–Oct)

## WATERSPORTS

It's a very small beach indeed that doesn't offer a few watersports facilities, such as pedaloes for hire, while older children might like to take lessons in windsurfing, available on most larger beaches.

 Pedaloes will delight children of all ages

# Sports & activities

In Ibiza you can lie on the beach doing nothing all day if you wish or you can exert all your night-time energies in the clubs. But if it's more conventional holiday activity you're after, then Ibiza has plenty of that too.

## CYCLING
Tourist offices can provide a leaflet covering biking routes, and bikes can be hired in almost every holiday resort. Formentera is great for cycling – you can rent bikes outside the ferry terminal (see page 85).
Ⓦ www.ibizacicloturismo.com

## DIVING
Ibiza has some of the cleanest waters in the Mediterranean, which makes for great diving with clear visibility. Explore submarine caves and a world of corals, colourful fish and sea anemones.

## GOLF
There is a golf course at Roca Llisa with separate 9- and 18-hole courses.
ⓐ Carretera Jesús-Cala Llonga, on the coast between Ibiza Town and Santa Eulària ⓣ 971 19 61 18 Ⓦ www.golfibiza.com
Ⓛ 08.30–20.00 daily

## HORSE RIDING
There are numerous stables on the island, including:
**Can Mayans** ⓐ Carretera Santa Gertrudis-Sant Llorenç ⓣ 971 18 73 88
Ⓛ 10.00–13.00, 17.00–until sunset daily
**Easy Rider** ⓐ Sol d'en Serra, 400 m (438 yds) from Cala Llonga beach
ⓣ 971 19 65 11 Ⓛ 10.00–13.00 & 17.00–until sunset daily

## INDOOR SPORTS
There are three municipal sports centres offering badminton, squash, indoor tennis and indoor or outdoor swimming pools.
ⓐ Polideportivo Municipal de Eivissa, Ibiza Town ⓣ 971 31 35 64

ⓐ Polideportivo Municipal Sant Antoni, Carretera Santa Agnes
ⓣ 971 34 54 02
ⓐ Polideportivo es Raspallar, Carretera Sant Antoni Km 1.5, Sa Blanca Dona
ⓣ 971 31 02 54 ⓛ 08.00–22.00 Mon–Fri, 08.00–12.00 Sat, closed Sun

## SAILING

There are sailing schools in Ibiza Town, Santa Eulària, San Antonio, Formentera and at many of the beaches. Throughout the year there are regattas, races and competitions for sailors.

**Anfibios** ⓐ Edificio Acapulco, opposite Space, Platja d'en Bossa
ⓣ 971 30 39 15 ⓦ www.anfibios.com ⓛ 09.00–19.00 Mon–Sat
(May–Oct), closed Sun

**Cesar's Water Sports** (see page 55) ⓐ S'Argamassa beach
ⓣ 971 33 09 19/670 62 99 61 ⓦ www.ibiza-spotlight.com/cesars
ⓛ 10.00–19.00 daily (May–Oct)

**Ibiza Mundo Activo** ⓐ Playa Niu Blau, Santa Eulària ⓣ 676 07 57 04
ⓦ www.ibizamundoactivo.com

**Julian and Oren** (see page 35) ⓐ Platja s'Arenal, Avinguda Doctor
Fleming, San Antonio ⓣ 971 34 65 35 ⓛ 08.00–22.00 daily

## WALKING

There are several waymarked trails starting from Santa Eulària, San Antonio, Platja d'en Bossa and Sant Miquel. Known as 'Falcon Routes', they lead to charming villages, secluded beaches or dramatic clifftops. At the start of the trails there is a board indicating the route and the level of difficulty. You can get leaflets from the tourist information office in Ibiza Town, San Antonio or Santa Eulària.

## WATERSPORTS

Most of the main beaches have some watersports facilities and there are at least 20 places with windsurfing equipment for hire. During the summer season, the winds are ideal for beginners; in the autumn they become stronger. The law in Spain requires an official licence in order to take charge of a motor boat, so you're unlikely to be given this choice.

# Festivals & events

### ART

Numerous artists have settled on, or visited, Ibiza over the years and
as a result there is a flourishing contemporary art scene. Strolling
around Ibiza Town you will see some of its many galleries. There is also
a small arts scene in Santa Eulària, with a couple of galleries there too:

ⓐ Galeria Alfredo, Carrer del Mar 4 ⓣ 971 33 00 47

ⓐ Galeria Cascais, Hotel Tres Torres, Passeig Marítim ⓣ 971 33 29 37

ⓦ www.hoteltrestorresibiza.com ⓛ 19.00–21.00 daily

🔺 Costumed characters during the medieval festival

## DANCING

Many hotels and restaurants put on flamenco displays, although flamenco is gypsy dancing from mainland Andalucía and not an Ibizan tradition. The island's dance is called *ball pages* and is thought to be at least 3,000 years old, having started as a pagan fertility dance. You can see it performed, and explained, every Thursday at about 18.00 in front of the church at Sant Miquel (the inland village and not the beach resort). There is also a small crafts market between 18.00 and 22.00.

## FESTIVALS

If you hear of a festival (*festa*) in your resort or at a nearby church or village, do make an effort to go along as you'll be made very welcome. Locals will appreciate your interest in their culture and you'll see a slice of real Ibizan life.

### May

During the summer season there's the **flower festival** in Santa Eulària on the first Sunday in May, and a **medieval festival** in Dalt Vila on the second weekend in May, celebrating the declaration of Ibiza Town as a World Heritage Site.

### June

The **Festival of Sant Joan** is on 24 June. This is celebrated with bonfires and fireworks, not only in the village of Sant Joan but elsewhere.

### July

On 16 July is the **Festival of Our Lady of Carmen**, who is the patron saint of sailors: boats are paraded and blessed, especially in Ibiza Town. On 25 July is the **Feast of Sant Jaume**, the patron saint of Formentera.

### August

From 1 to 8 August are the **Festival of the Earth** (Festes de la Terra); the **Festival of Our Lady of the Snows**, the patron saint of these pine islands;

⏷ *Fireworks over Ibiza Town during the Festival of Sant Ciriaco*

and the **Festival of Sant Ciriaco**, patron saint of Ibiza Town. This develops into one long party, culminating in a fireworks display.

A big summer festival on 24 August is the **Festival of Sant Bartolomeu** in San Antonio with fireworks and music.

### September

On 8 September is the last big summer festival, the **Fiesta of Jesús** in Santa Eulària, a religious festival with traditional dance.

Every year in the third week of September there is a **Tourist Festival**. Hotels and town halls arrange free excursions or tours, special dances and food tasting. Ask for further information at the tourist offices.

▶ *Ibiza is clearly signposted*

# PRACTICAL INFORMATION
Tips & advice

# Accommodation

### HOTELS IN IBIZA

In some of the towns, you can find *hostals*. These are not youth hostels with shared facilities but family-run, bed-and-breakfast-style hotels. There are numerous reasonably priced *hostals* in San Antonio, while in the bay the majority of the accommodation is in apartments; these two areas tend to be the cheapest on the island. Around Ibiza Town, accommodation tends to be more expensive.

There is a new wave of hotels on the island known as *agroturismos*. These tend to be more exclusive hotels out in the countryside, and often run as a kind of retreat with spas and chic lounge bars.

Pop in to **Everything Ibiza**, a travel agency and information service, for last-minute bookings. Especially good for *hostals* in San Antonio. ⓐ Avinguda Doctor Fleming 9 (near the Egg roundabout) ① 971 80 36 80 ⓦ www.everythingibiza.com

Price ratings are based on a double room for one night:
£ = up to €75    ££ = €75–€150    £££ = over €150

**Hostal Las Arenas £–££** All rooms in this little *hostal*, located right in the middle of Es Canar overlooking the end of the bay, have private bathrooms and air-conditioning. Breakfast is included. ⓐ Es Canar by the port ① 971 33 07 90 ⓦ www.lasarenasibiza.com

**Ca's Català ££** English-owned small hotel near Santa Eulària's old church and a short walk into town. There's a bar and swimming pool in the walled garden. ⓐ Carrer del Sol, Santa Eulària ① 971 33 10 06 ⓦ www.cascatala.com

**Fiesta Hotel Palmyra ££** Next to the port and overlooking the beachfront promenade, the Palmyra hotel is close to San Antonio but far enough away to avoid the noise. Relax by the pool, or in the large lounges, and enjoy the comfortable rooms with air-conditioning and sea views.

ⓐ Avinguda Dr Fleming, San Antonio ⓣ 971 34 03 54
ⓦ www.fiestahotelgroup.com

**Garbi Aparthotel ££** This apartment-hotel is popular with families. Garbi has tennis courts, squash courts, its own supermarket, and a disco right on the beach. With a packed programme of evening entertainment you may never leave the complex. ⓐ Carrer de Murtra, Platja d'en Bossa ⓣ 971 30 00 07 ⓦ www.hotelgarbi-ibiza.com

**Hostal Parque ££** Right on the pedestrianised Plaça des Parc and next to Dalt Vila, this *hostal* is the perfect spot for a quick break to Ibiza Town. All rooms are air-conditioned; double rooms have modern en-suite bathrooms. ⓐ Plaça des Parc 4, Ibiza Town ⓣ 971 30 13 58 ⓦ www.hostalparque.com

**Hotel Hawaii Ibiza ££** The newly extended Passeig Marítim runs in front of the hotel so you can stroll along the promenade to San Antonio, and you have all the bars and restaurants of the bay right on your doorstep. ⓐ Carrer s'Embarcador, Punta de's Molí, San Antonio Bay ⓣ 971 34 05 62 ⓦ www.intertur.es

**Hotel Marfil ££** Air-conditioned rooms and wi-fi in each room make this *hostal* excellent value for money. You can use the pool at the neighbouring sister hotel, Tarba. Breakfast included. ⓐ Carrer Ramón y Cajal 34, San Antonio ⓣ 971 34 12 08 ⓦ www.hotelmarfil.com

**Hotel Hacienda Na Xamena £££** This Indian-influenced hacienda in the pine-strewn hills overlooks a stunning cove surrounded by sheer cliffs. Ibiza's first five-star hotel boasts a thalasso-spa and a massaging waterfall pool high on the cliff face, an outdoor pool and two restaurants. Rooms are spread over several levels, and some suites even have their own private mini-pool overlooking the bay. ⓐ Na Xamena, Sant Miquel ⓣ 971 33 45 00 ⓦ www.hotelhacienda-ibiza.com

# Preparing to go

## GETTING THERE

The cheapest way to get to Ibiza is to book a package holiday with one of the leading tour operators specialising in Ibiza holidays. You should also check the travel supplements of the weekend newspapers for special deals. If your travelling times are flexible, and you can avoid the school holidays, you may find some very cheap last-minute deals. Some of the main tour operators are:

Ⓦ www.lastminute.com
Ⓦ www.thomascook.com

## By air

Flight times to Ibiza from the UK are approximately two hours.
For bookings you may want to visit the following websites:

Ⓦ www.easyjet.com
Ⓦ www.flythomascook.com
Ⓦ www.skyscanner.net
Ⓦ www.travelsupermarket.com

Many people are aware that air travel emits $CO_2$, which contributes to climate change. You may be interested in the possibility of lessening the environmental impact of your flight through the charity Climate Care, which offsets your $CO_2$ by funding environmental projects around the world. Visit Ⓦ www.jpmorganclimatecare.com

## By ferry
### Ibiza

Ferries leave from the ports at Valencia and Barcelona, as well as Palma de Mallorca, sometimes offering really cheap deals at the end of the season.

Trasmediterranea's (Ⓦ www.trasmediterranea.es) UK agent is Southern Ferries (ⓐ 30 Churton Street, London SW1V 2LP ⓣ 0844 815 7785 Ⓦ www.southernferries.co.uk). Early bookings are necessary for school holidays, and pensioners can receive a 20 per cent discount.

### Formentera

On arrival at Ibiza Airport, head to Ibiza Town for the ferry (see page 85). **Balearia** car ferries leave from the Ibiza Old Town end of the port and need booking in advance. ☎ 902 16 01 80 🅦 www.balearia.com

## TOURISM AUTHORITY
### Spanish Tourist Office
#### UK
ⓐ 2nd floor, 29 New Cavendish St, London W1W 6XB ☎ 0870 850 6599/020 7317 2010 🅦 www.spain.info/uk/TourSpain

For information on resorts, contact the following local tourist offices.

### Ibiza Town
ⓐ Passeig Vara del Rey 1 🅦 www.ibiza.travel/en

### Casa de la Curia (Ibiza Town)
ⓐ Plaça de la Catedral ☎ 971 39 92 32 🅦 www.ibiza.travel/en

### Port of Ibiza
ⓐ Carrer Antoni Riquer 2 ☎ 971 19 19 51

### Figueretes
ⓐ Passeig de Julià Verdera 🕒 Jun–Oct

### Ibiza Airport
ⓐ Arrivals hall ☎ 971 80 91 18

### Sant Antoni de Portmany
ⓐ Passeig de ses Fonts ☎ 971 34 33 63 🅦 www.santantoni.net

### Santa Eulària
ⓐ Carrer Mariano Riquer 4 ☎ 971 33 07 28 🅦 www.santaeulalia.net

### Formentera
ⓐ Plaça de la Constitució 1, Sant Francesc ☎ 971 32 20 57 🅦 www.turismoformentera.com

## BEFORE YOU LEAVE

It is not necessary to have inoculations to travel in Europe, but you should make sure that you and your family are up to date with the basics, such as tetanus. It is a good idea to pack a small first-aid kit to carry with you containing plasters, antiseptic cream, travel sickness pills, insect repellent and/or bite relief cream, antihistamine tablets, upset stomach remedies and painkillers. Sun lotion can be more expensive in Ibiza so it is worth taking a good selection, and don't forget after-sun cream as well. If you are taking prescription medicines, ensure that you take enough for the duration of your visit – you may find it impossible to obtain the same medicines in Ibiza. It is also worth having a dental check-up before you go.

## ENTRY FORMALITIES
### Passports & visas

Citizens of the UK, Republic of Ireland and other EU countries only require a valid up-to-date passport. Check well in advance that your passport is up to date and has at least three months left to run. All children, including newborn babies, need their own passport now, unless they are already included on the passport of the person they are travelling with.

### TRAVEL INSURANCE

Do you have sufficient insurance cover for your holiday? Check that your policy covers you adequately for loss of possessions and valuables, for activities you might want to try – such as scuba-diving, horse riding or watersports – and for emergency medical and dental treatment, including flights home, if required.

For EU residents, make sure you have your EHIC card (this replaces the E111 form), which allows EU visitors access to reduced cost, and sometimes free, state-provided medical treatment in the European Economic Area (EEA). For further information, ring the EHIC enquiries line (☎ 0845 605 0707) or visit the UK Department of Health website (🌐 www.ehic.org.uk).

For citizens of the USA, Canada, Australia, New Zealand and South Africa, if you are staying less than 90 days a visa is not required.

## Customs and duty-free allowances

There is no limit to the amount of goods you can bring back into EU countries from Spain; however, if you have a large amount you may be stopped by customs and asked what you are buying it for.

For non-EU countries (and this includes the Channel Islands, Gibraltar and the Canary Islands), travellers over the age of 17 can take back 200 cigarettes or 250 g of other tobacco products, 4 litres of wine, 16 litres of beer and €430 of other goods and souvenirs.

The official website for the UK Customs & Excise is
ⓦ www.hmce.gov.uk

## MONEY

In line with the majority of EU member states, Spain entered the single currency on 1 January 2002. Euro note denominations are: 500, 200, 100, 50, 20, 10 and 5. Coins are 1 and 2 euros and 1, 2, 5, 10, 20 and 50 céntimos.

ATMs (cashpoint machines) are found throughout Ibiza and Formentera, especially in the larger towns of Ibiza, Santa Eulària and San Antonio, but you may have to travel to find one if you are staying in a quiet beach area. For payment in stores and restaurants, you will need to know your PIN (personal identification number), and often you will also be asked for photo identity.

Widely used in the tourist resorts (check with a restaurant before you sit down), credit cards can also be used as a deposit on car hire. If you run short of cash, you may be able to get money on your credit card at one of the major banks or at a cashpoint.

You can change traveller's cheques and sterling at any bank, or at travel agencies, exchange bureaux, larger hotels and some shops, although banks give better rates. Look for the Cambio sign. You will need you passport when cashing traveller's cheques.

◆ *Springtime in Ibiza*

## CLIMATE

Summers are warm and tend to be dry from June, with temperatures reaching more than 30°C (85°F) in August and September. Summer clothing is advisable, although a light jacket is recommended in the early hours due to the humidity of the island. From September, a light raincoat is a good idea in case of autumn storms, which last only a few hours. Winter temperatures drop quite low at night, rising to just over 20°C (70°F) during the day. This can be a lovely time of year to come, although it can be very quiet as many establishments close from October to the end of April.

## BAGGAGE ALLOWANCES

Baggage allowances vary according to the airline, destination and the class of travel, but 20 kg (44 lb) per person is the norm for luggage carried in the hold (you can normally find your luggage allowance printed on your airline ticket). Check if you are booked onto one of the budget airlines, as you may find you should be paying extra for hold luggage and that it should have been booked in advance.

Generally, you are allowed one item of cabin baggage weighing no more than 5 kg (11 lb), and measuring 46 by 30 by 23 cm (18 by 12 by 9 in). In addition, you can usually carry your airport purchases, as well as umbrella, handbag, coat, camera, etc., as hand baggage, although, due to recent changes in hand luggage, you are often asked to bring only one item. Check with the airline about the current hand luggage restrictions.

You can find further information on the UK Department for Transport website (W www.dft.gov.uk). Large items – surfboards, golf clubs, collapsible wheelchairs and pushchairs – are usually charged as extras, and it is a good idea to let the airline know in advance if you want to bring these.

# During your stay

## AIRPORTS

Ibiza has only one airport, which is located 8 km (5 miles) away from Ibiza Town (❶ 902 40 47 04). Because the island is so small, it is no more than an hour's drive to the furthest resort.

The majority of visitors use charter airlines to get to Ibiza, and these operate from most of the UK's airports. Ibiza's modern airport is also served by scheduled international flights from the UK and by internal flights from Spanish airports at Madrid, Valencia and Barcelona.

Car hire is available and is best booked in advance from home where you can get better deals by pre-booking.

**Avis** Ⓦ www.avis.com
**Europcar** Ⓦ www.europcar.com
**Hertz** Ⓦ www.hertz.com
**Hipercar** Ⓦ www.hiperrentacar.com
**Travel Supermarket** Ⓦ www.travelsupermarket.com

### Taxis

Taxis from the airport to Ibiza Town and Platja d'en Bossa area cost around €15, while a taxi to Santa Eulària or San Antonio might cost about €30.
ⓐ Radio Taxi de San José ❶ 971 80 00 80

### Buses

Ibiza Bus runs several buses to the airport.
No 9 Sant Antoni–Sant Josep–Airport (every 45 mins).
No 10 Ibiza Town–Airport (every 20 mins).
No 10B Ibiza Town–Platja d'en Bossa–Airport (every 60 mins).
No 24 Es Canar–Santa Eulària–Airport (every 2 hours).
See Ⓦ www.ibizabus.com for details.

## COMMUNICATIONS
### Telephones

Public telephones work well, and usually have instructions in several

languages. Stock up with coins or, much easier, buy a phonecard for €6 or €12 at a *tabacos* (tobacconist), a shop or a hotel. Lots of bars and restaurants also have payphones. In the major towns of Ibiza, San Antonio and Santa Eulària, there are special telephone shops or *locutorios* where you can make your call, local or international, and pay for it afterwards.

To make a local call, ring the nine-figure number listed. All numbers throughout the Balearic Islands are prefixed with the code 971. If you want to use your mobile phone while on holiday, check with your provider for international roaming set-up and rates.

## Post offices

Post offices are normally open 08.30–20.30 Mon–Fri and 08.30–14.00 Sat; there are main post offices in Ibiza Town, San Antonio and Santa Eulària (look for the Correos sign). Elsewhere you can often buy stamps at tobacconists (look for the Tabacos sign). Official postboxes are a distinctive yellow, but remember that most hotel receptions will send cards for you. See ⓦ www.correos.es for details.

---

**TELEPHONING IBIZA FROM ABROAD**
Dial the international access code (00), 34 (Spain's country code), then the nine-digit number.

**TELEPHONING ABROAD**
Australia: 00 61 + area code (minus the 0) + telephone number
New Zealand: 00 64 + area code (minus the 0) + telephone number
Republic of Ireland: 00 353 + area code (minus the 0) + telephone number
South Africa: 00 27 + area code (minus the 0) + telephone number
UK: 00 44 + area code (minus the 0) + telephone number
United States and Canada: 00 1 + area code (minus the 0) + telephone number

### Internet & wi-fi

Many bars, restaurants and hotels have internet access with one or two terminals you can use. In Ibiza Town and Santa Eulària, several internet stores have up to 20 terminals. Wi-fi access is also becoming more popular throughout the island, with hotels, bars and cafés in many resorts offering the service free to paying customers. Ask at the tourist office for addresses.

## DRESS CODES

Pretty much anything goes in Ibiza. There are very few dress codes in any of the resorts. However, if you are going to one of the restaurants in town, or to Pacha and El Divino clubs, check to see what is appropriate. Pacha and El Divino clubs tend to be a little stricter when it comes to men's clothing, and you might find you're not able to enter if you are wearing shorts.

## ELECTRICITY

Electricity is 220 V all over the island and two-pin plugs are used. Adaptors can be found both in hotel receptions and in souvenir shops. If you are considering buying electrical appliances to take home, always check that they will work in your country of residence before you buy.

## EMERGENCIES
### Hospitals
**Hospital Can Misses** Ibiza and Formentera's main hospital is just outside Ibiza and has a 24-hour emergency service.
ⓐ Intersection between Avinguda de la Pau and Carrer de la Corona, Ibiza Town ⓣ 971 39 70 00 ⓦ www.hcm-ibiza.es

### Pharmacies

For minor medical ailments, visit a *farmàcia* (pharmacy). Look for a green cross. There is always a pharmacy open 24 hours a day (*farmàcia de guardia*). Every pharmacy will have a notice indicating which pharmacy is on duty at which time.

**EMERGENCY NUMBER**
**Ambulance, fire and police:** dial 112

## Consulates

If you lose your passport and need help, contact your consulate. Note that they will be unable to help with any financial matters other than contacting someone in your home country who might be able to send money over in an emergency.

### Australia

ⓐ Torre Espacio, Paseo de la Castellana, 259D, Planta 24, 28046 Madrid
ⓣ 913 53 66 00

### Canada

ⓐ Calle Nuñez de Balboa 35, 28001 Madrid ⓣ 914 23 32 50

### New Zealand

ⓐ Pinar 7, 3rd floor, 28014 Madrid ⓣ 915 23 02 26

### Republic of Ireland

ⓐ Carrer Sant Miquel 68A, 07002 Palma de Mallorca ⓣ 971 71 92 44

### South Africa

ⓐ Calle Claudio Coello 91, 28006 Madrid ⓣ 914 36 37 80

### UK Vice-Consulate

ⓐ Avinguda d'Isidor Macabich 45, 1st floor, 07800 Ibiza ⓣ 971 30 18 18

### US Consulate

ⓐ Edificio Reina Constanza, Porto Pi, 8, Palma de Mallorca ⓣ 971 40 37 07

## GETTING AROUND
### Car hire
Car hire is a popular way of getting around the island, and rates are very competitive. Most resorts and towns have car hire offices that you can pop into. You can rent a car by the day, which usually means that you have it for 24 hours. Spain has one of the worst records for road accidents in Europe, so do take care and don't take chances. As a foreigner in a hired car you will probably get the blame for any accident, so you may want to consider paying that little bit extra for full insurance.

Speed limits are 50 km/h (31 mph) in towns, 90 km/h (56 mph) on main roads outside towns and 100 km/h (62 mph) on *autovias* (four or more lanes). Spanish police often mount speed traps and have the power to make on-the-spot fines. Check the parking restrictions before you leave the car. Blue lines often mean it is metered parking, so look for a meter nearby and make sure you have change.

### Mopeds, motorbikes & quad bikes
There are mopeds, motorbikes and quad bikes for hire in all the main resorts, and they are a cheap way of getting to out-of-the-way beaches. Accidents happen, though, so take care. If you're 16 or over, you can rent a machine under 49 cc – you have to be 18 to hire one that's 75 cc or over. Crash helmets are compulsory, and ensure you have adequate insurance cover.

### Public transport
### Buses
The good news is that buses on Ibiza are very cheap and can get you to most places on the island. The bad news is that some can be crowded. Ibiza Town is the hub and the bus station is on Avinguda d'Isidor Macabich. San Antonio also has a large bus station. Ibiza Bus company puts on the Discobus (see page 70) that takes you to all the big clubs and between San Antonio and Ibiza Town.
Ⓦ www.ibizabus.com

 A lone scooter at Cala Conta beach

## Boats & ferries

In San Antonio and Ibiza Town you can hop on a boat that goes to
just about any of the nearby beaches. There are regular ferries from
Ibiza Town across to the Spanish mainland, to Palma de Mallorca and
to the neighbouring island of Formentera, a popular day trip
(see page 85).

## Taxis

The sticker saying 'SP' on the front and back bumpers of cars doesn't
mean Spain; it means 'Servicio Público', or public service vehicle. A green
light on the roof above the driver's seat means the taxi is for hire. You
can usually find a list of the fixed prices attached to a post next to the
taxi rank to give you a guideline. Taxis between San Antonio and Ibiza
Town can cost around €30.

A 10 per cent tip is about right. All taxi drivers have a permit number,
so make a note of it in the unlikely event of any disagreement, in which
case a receipt will be needed.

**Ibiza Town** ☎ 971 39 84 83
**San Antonio** ☎ 971 34 37 64
**Santa Eulària** ☎ 971 33 00 63
**Formentera** ☎ 971 32 20 16

## HEALTH, SAFETY & CRIME

Crime is not a major problem in Ibiza by any means, but watch out for
pickpockets and bag-snatchers in markets, bus stations and other
crowded places. It is illegal for flowers or tickets to be sold in the street,
and do not be tempted by games in the street – they are rigged!

Don't take anything valuable to the beach or leave it lying around
when you go for a swim. Likewise, if you hire a car, try not to leave any
bags where people can see them.

The possession of drugs is illegal in Ibiza and can be subject to
imprisonment. There is a small drugs problem, and occasional muggings
have happened by people desperate for money. Try not to be on your own
late at night.

If you lose something, report it to the police or the Guardia Civil (Civil Guard). The vast majority of Ibicencos are honest and will hand in any lost property. If you have children and one of them wanders away from you, just ask for help in the nearest bar, restaurant, hotel or shop, or go to the nearest police or Guardia Civil station, which is where lost children should be taken.

Avoid sun exposure between 13.00 and 16.00, and use high sun protection factor (SPF) lotions in order to prevent sunburn, especially in children.

## MEDIA

International newspapers are available in Ibiza Town and some resorts. The local newspapers are *Diario de Ibiza* (W www.diariodeibiza.es) and *Ultima Hora de Ibiza y Formentera* (W www.ultimahora.es/ibiza). Also see the English-language online newspaper W www.theibizasun.com

## OPENING HOURS

Beach bars tend to stay open all day serving teas, coffees and drinks, while the kitchen opens around lunchtime, closing approximately 16.00–19.00 and then reopening until 24.00 or 01.00.

Banks and post offices are mostly only open in the mornings, 09.00–14.00 Monday to Saturday.

Shops in town tend to open 09.00–14.00 and reopen around 17.00–22.00; some smaller supermarkets in the resorts may stay open all day and as late as 23.00 in the busy summer months.

## RELIGION

The English-speaking church of Ibiza holds several services in Sant Rafel and Santa Eulària on alternating Sundays, with a Sunday School at 11.00 during the summer months.
T 971 34 44 83 W www.ibizachurch.com

## TIME DIFFERENCES

Ibiza is one hour ahead of GMT. As in the UK, clocks go forward one hour on the last Sunday in March and go back one hour on the last Sunday in

October. Add or subtract the given number of hours to or from Spanish time to get the time in each country.

**Australia** +8 hours
**New Zealand** +10 hours
**United Kingdom** +1 hour
**US Eastern Time** −6 hours
**US Pacific Time** −9 hours

## TIPPING

How much and whether to tip is entirely a matter of personal choice, although a tip of around 10 per cent for taxis and restaurants might be considered. In bars, often just a few cents or rounding the bill up to the nearest euro is fair.

## TOILETS

In general, toilets in Ibiza are very good. All bars and restaurants have toilet and washroom facilities of high standards.

## TRAVELLERS WITH DISABILITIES

Wheelchairs can be rented in Ortofarma Tur Viñas, Ibiza Town (ⓐ Avinguda España 6 ⓣ 971 39 28 91 ⓛ 10.00–13.30, 17.00–21.00 Mon–Sat). Electric wheelchairs can be hired from Farmàcia Ramia-Planas (ⓐ Avinguda d'Espanya 36 ⓣ 971 30 13 79). Access to shops, restaurants and hotels varies. Many more expensive establishments are well equipped for people with disabilities. Some of the less expensive establishments have no lifts or may have numerous steps. It is advisable to check with each individual location before you arrive. Also note that some of the beach bars and restaurants in the smaller resorts will not be wheelchair accessible as you can only reach them via the sand.

## ACKNOWLEDGEMENTS

The publishers would like to thank the following for providing their copyright photographs for this book: DREAMSTIME C. Nitu pages 19, 52, 71, Tamas pages 10, 74, J. Vanden Borre page 52, V. Rus page 107, V. Barcelo Varona page 67; Fiona Quinn pages 21, 29, 61; FLICKER Gavin White page 44, Fabio Rezzola page 87, Juliet Roddy-Stevenson pages 55, 84, 88; Geoff Williamson Image Collection page 114; Pictures Colour Library Ltd pages 30, 80, 82, 95, 106; Thomas Cook Tour Operations Ltd pages 5, 13, 16, 25, 27, 35, 38, 49, 59, 64, 68, 72, 79, 91, 92; World Pictures pages 98, 101, 104, 121.

Project editor: Tom Willsher
Layout: Donna Pedley
Proofreader: Karolin Thomas
Indexer: Marie Lorimer

Send your thoughts to
# books@thomascook.com

- Found a beach bar, peaceful stretch of sand or must-see sight that we don't feature?

- Like to tip us off about any information that needs a little updating?

- Want to tell us what you love about this handy little guidebook and more importantly how we can make it even handier?

Then here's your chance to tell all! Send us ideas, discoveries and recommendations today and then look out for your valuable input in the next edition of this title.

Email to the above address or write to:
pocket guides Series Editor, Thomas Cook Publishing, PO Box 227, Coningsby Road, Peterborough PE3 8SB, UK.

# Useful phrases

| English | Spanish | Approx pronunciation |
|---|---|---|
| **BASICS** | | |
| **Yes** | Sí | Si |
| **No** | No | Noh |
| **Please** | Por favor | Por fabor |
| **Thank you** | Gracias | Grathias |
| **Hello** | Hola | Ola |
| **Goodbye** | Adiós | Adios |
| **Excuse me** | Disculpe | Diskoolpeh |
| **Sorry** | Perdón | Pairdohn |
| **That's okay** | De acuerdo | Dey acwerdo |
| **I don't speak Spanish** | No hablo español | Noh ablo espanyol |
| **Do you speak English?** | ¿Habla usted inglés? | ¿Abla oosteth eengless? |
| **Good morning** | Buenos días | Bwenos dee-as |
| **Good afternoon** | Buenas tardes | Bwenas tarrdess |
| **Good evening** | Buenas noches | Bwenas notchess |
| **Goodnight** | Buenas noches | Bwenas notchess |
| **My name is ...** | Me llamo ... | Meh yiamo ... |
| **NUMBERS** | | |
| **One** | Uno | Oono |
| **Two** | Dos | Dos |
| **Three** | Tres | Tres |
| **Four** | Cuatro | Cwatro |
| **Five** | Cinco | Thinco |
| **Six** | Seis | Seys |
| **Seven** | Siete | Seeyetey |
| **Eight** | Ocho | Ocho |
| **Nine** | Nueve | Nwebeyh |
| **Ten** | Diez | Deeyeth |
| **Twenty** | Veinte | Beintey |
| **Fifty** | Cincuenta | Thincwenta |
| **One hundred** | Cien | Thien |
| **SIGNS & NOTICES** | | |
| **Airport** | Aeropuerto | Aehropwerto |
| **Rail station** | Estación de trenes | Estathion de trenes |
| **Platform** | Vía | Via |
| **Smoking/** | Fumadores/ | Foomadoores/ |
| **Non-smoking** | No fumadores | No foomadores |
| **Toilets** | Servicios | Serbitheeos |
| **Ladies/Gentlemen** | Señoras/Caballeros | Senyoras/Kabayeros |